Advance

"Now, more than ever, people are looking for the push. The motivation to become their own best version. The stimulation and the catalyst to ignore limits and go beyond, become unstoppable, create legacies. Laura's book is that push you have been looking for. A fascinating read, an extraordinary woman."

– Mirav Tarkka, Book mentor, bestselling author and publisher, psychologist & criminologist.

"Revamped is a light-hearted self-help book that gets you back on track to take control of your life again. As an account of personal growth despite trauma, it is inspiring and reminded me that I too deserve to be happy. And isn't that what John Lennon wanted to be when he grew up?"

– Jessica Sankala, Entrepreneur, vibrational essence maven & indecently divine enchantress.

"Laura has used her traumatic experience to shift her into another gear. She now lives her life to the full and that's what she wants for you, to life your best life. She will show you how"

– Ann Guindi, Entrepreneur, Author, Speaker & Award Winning Coach

"Reading Laura's words is literally like watching a movie. She has that way of writing that will make you picture every scene and make you feel every emotion.

You will only regret one thing as you read her novel : that it has an end!"

– Pauline Lobe Ollo Enangue, Bestselling Author & Holistic Womb Wellness Mentor, Yoni Steam Practitioner & Teacher

REVAMPED

Laura

BERGGREN

LEGAL DISCLAIMER

The entire content of REVAMPED, must be considered as exclusively informative and cannot in any way be understood as a substitute, alternative or supplementary of professional opinions or medical consultations, nor refer to specific individual cases, for which we invite you to consult your own attending physician and / or recognized specialists. The contents of REVAMPD are for informational purposes only and should not be intended to treat, diagnose, prevent or treat any ailment or disease. The author of this work decline any responsibility for any consequences deriving from a use of its contents other than merely informative.

Nothing contained in this work constitutes or intends to constitute a suggestion of any nature. If the user of REVAMPED feels the need for advice in relation to any topic, you are invited to contact a qualified professional in the specific field.

If the reader of REVAMPED suspects or is aware of having or having had or being exposed to problems, disturbances and / or physical or psychological illnesses and in any case in any case, must rely on appropriate medical treatment recommended by a professional of their own trust.

Despite the scrupulous care used in the preparation of REVAMPED, drawn up with the utmost accuracy and diligence, it is not possible ensure that the information contained within it is free from errors, omissions or inaccuracies.

Laura Berggren disclaim any liability, direct and indirect, towards readers, regarding inaccuracies, errors, omissions, damages, deriving from the aforementioned contents.

The author of REVAMPED cannot guarantee the users of the book to obtain the same results of personal, character growth, psychological, motivational, physical or any other nature or denomination on a par with as set out in this work.

Within REVAMPED the ideas of consultants and experts are cited and hosted which in an absolutely free form, not constituting what they affirmed an opinion of a professional or similar nature, offered their contribution for information purposes only, without any presumption or willingness to place oneself above the recognized traditional medical system. It is at the free discretion of the user of REVAMPED and its absolute responsibility for any willingness to follow or replicate some of the advice proposed therein or to contact other competent personnel, according to your own beliefs, knowledge, habits and wills.

Everything included within REVAMPED must always be understood as the subjective opinion of the author, given that these considerations can also run counter to the precepts of knowledge taught in universities and / or in the scientific world and therefore go there considered as simple expressions or controversies of a personal and in any case non-professional nature, having to make exclusive reference to/and reliance solely on traditional and recognized fields of knowledge.

COPYRIGHTS

For anyone craving a life of fulfillment, searching for something more or simply in need of a redo.

Table of Contents

INTRODUCTION

The Journey to Becoming...

It all started with me wanting to write a book on helping you become the best version of yourself and live your best possible life, until I realized I wasn't doing that myself. Who was I to offer tangible advice and tips on how to do the very thing I wasn't? Wouldn't that make me an imposter? A fake? Who would listen to someone who still allowed their mind to take over? Who still welcomed their external circumstances to run their life from time to time? But then, it all dawned on me.

Wouldn't that just make me more real and relatable? I mean, who really has their life all figured out? Is anyone REALLY living their best life? I feel we're always called to do more, especially once we've reached so-called "success". So then, why couldn't I? Was there anything wrong with sharing with others what I've learned so far along the way to living my best life? We can travel the journey together and learn as we go and not feel so alone. Like a couple of best friends going on a road trip. Just hopping in the car and going, no destination planned and see where the road takes us. In my eyes, there is absolutely nothing wrong with that at all!

I want you to look at this book as two friends, you and me, chatting about life. Maybe over a coffee or a nice glass of expensive wine. Discussing all the things, good and bad that life throws at us. After all, in order to live our best lives, don't we have to appreciate all the good and bad times it brings?

Some of the things I share you may agree or relate to, other times it could be the exact opposite and you know what, that is okay. We're all unique in our own way and what works or resonates with one person may not with another. I'm sure you can relate to times in life you found this to be true.

So, if you take away anything from this book, I hope it's simply to not give up on what is tugging at your heart and calling for you to do and to find fulfillment in every day. Had I listened to myself, this book would have never been published. Even if it only helps or changes one person, it's done its purpose. Let's buckle up and begin enjoying the journey to living your best life.

CHAPTER ONE

What Is Standing In Your Way?

"The only person standing in your way is you."
– Vincent Cassel

I'll never forget the day that forever changed my life. It was a cold and rainy November day, nothing out of the ordinary for this time of year. When the car I was in hydroplaned, sending us into a whirlwind of spins on the highway, traffic barreling towards us at rapid speeds. I remember life flashing before my eyes. For those of you that have ever been in this situation, knows that this happens very slowly. And although, the external circumstance is over in a matter of seconds, it feels like an eternity, waiting to see if you're going to survive the impact or not.

Clearly, I survived if I'm here today to tell you about it. In fact, I walked away from it, surprisingly with no injuries. Why am I even telling you this and how is it relevant to living your best life? Well, sometimes it takes experiencing trauma or a near death experience to wake you up and realize just how short life really is. That your expiration date could come at any time.

Funny enough, but not humorous in any way, experiencing this traumatic event didn't wake me up and it should have. It ought to make me reassess my life, the people that were a part of it and the goals I hadn't yet accomplished or even made a plan to begin working towards. I really didn't think I was going to survive this and it should have WOKE ME THE FUCK UP. But it didn't.

My girls were soon going to be on their way home from school on the bus and all I could envision was someone meeting them at the stop and telling them that Mommy wasn't coming home. It still to this day, five years later, brings tears to my eyes and makes me sick to my stomach when I think about that. Currently, as I'm writing these words, the waterworks have begun. I can't imagine not being here for them. They are my world.

So, why didn't it shake me, make me change my ways and open my eyes? I'm not entirely sure. It didn't really affect me until present day when I was listening to a podcast talking about our expiration date. It hit me in such a way, I can't even explain. Again, the tears came pouring out, as recollection of the accident vividly appeared in my mind. It was then, that I realized how extremely lucky I was to have a second chance to do life the way I truly wanted to. That is when my life changed.

We all have an expiration date. When you really sit back and think about how limited our time here really is, you wouldn't let some of the small, petty stuff bother you. In all honesty, we really don't know when our last day here is. It could be in 40 years, a couple of months, maybe even tomorrow.

When the end of your life is a big question mark, it doesn't leave much room for error. There's not a whole lot of time available to settle, be unhappy and unfulfilled. So, why do you suppose so many of us do that then? Wasting many countless days of our precious life, not doing what we wish we could. Not living out what's on our hearts.

Your time matters. We all have our definition of hectic and if you think about all the things we do in our day, how much of it is wasted time? We're busy being parents or care givers of some sort, going to school and work. I totally get it. But, how do you suppose Oprah fits it all in? We all get the same twenty-four hours.

Often times we pour out so much into others that we don't make the time we should for ourselves. You need to keep doing those things that are important to you. What can be beneficial to your choices, your decisions and priorities? When life begins to become busier than ever, start asking yourself if you're scheduling in time for you. Are you making healthier choices for your mind, body and soul? Are you setting yourself up for success?

Throughout life we go through many trial and errors. We make mistakes and we say things we don't really mean. We let people go that we thought would be in our lives forever and we experience moments that wake us the fuck up, both good and bad. You know why I didn't change my life back then? I made excuses. There was other things to do. I told myself it wasn't for me. I got in my own damn way.

Now, stay with me here for a second. If you were to envision your absolute best life, what would you see? What would you smell? What would you hear? Do you taste anything? Who do you picture yourself surrounded by?

Let's just for a minute close our eyes and lose ourselves in that moment. I want you to feel it around you. Fall into it. Embrace it. Picture it. Just let go. It's alright, go ahead, I'll wait.

Ah ha! Busted! You didn't do it, did you? No seriously, I want you to try this. I feel it's something that is extremely important. You need to let lose for a minute and picture yourself living your best life.

Okay, now as you open your eyes and look around at your current surroundings, do you have any immediate new feelings come upon you? Do you feel like you're almost stuck? Are you suddenly missing what you pictured? Do you feel unhappy or like you're settling? Are you already picturing changes that need to be made?

Then let's go for it!

Do everything you've ever desired to do. Find a way to make it possible. Work jobs in different countries if that's something on your heart. Talk to your crush. Change careers. I think the absolute biggest secret is to live life with no regrets. When you get to the end of your days and you look back, you'll see that you did and accomplished everything you wanted to do and try, even if it didn't go as planned. There's nothing left undone.

You remembered to live. You remembered to smile. To find gratitude in every day. To be thankful for so many things. To always look towards the positive. To not let anyone hold you back. To surround yourself with people who lift you higher and only want the best for you. To not care what others think and take advice from everyone but only implement the advice from those who have already achieved what you're going after and are successful. To step out of your comfort zone and not be afraid. Face your fears. Travel the world, see new places, meet new people and learn all the things. But also, to never forget to take care of yourself first. Exercise and eat good food. Fall in love. Hug more people. Don't read too much into what you see in the news or on social media. Find the good in every day. Be happy. (You really deserve to be happy!) Be authentically you. Be true to yourself. You're limited edition baby!

And that, that is how you live your best life. THE END.

No, I'm just kidding. We're only getting started, but this my friend, is where your story begins.

It's all up to you!

I've previously mentioned some great examples of things I feel are needed to live your best life, but we're going to dive in even deeper. Get to the root of it all and find tactical strategies you can implement to continue living your best life each and every day.

So, let's start at the very beginning. Typically when we don't feel like we're living our best life it's because someone is standing in our way. No, it's not your parents, your spouse or your kids, although all of those can play a huge factor in how you live your life, it's not the one we're looking for here. It's YOU! You're the ONLY ONE standing in your own damn way!

YOU are the only one that makes a variety of decisions about your life. What you wear. Who you're friends with. Who you date. Where you work. How you feel. What you're thinking. ALL YOU! Seeing a pattern here? Now, don't get me wrong, I'm aware of the many influences that can pop in and out and shuffle things up a bit or alter the direction you were planning on heading. We'll get to some of those later on.

The bottom line is, YOU ARE responsible for all the choices you make in your life, even if you feel like the choice isn't yours. Sorry, for all the caps, I just want to make sure this is sticking. Who's responsible for living their best life? YOU! Who's the only one that has any control over how your life will turn out? That's right – YOU! Who wants to join me on the beach somewhere exotic chatting over piña coladas? I'm hoping YOU!

So, now that we have established that your life is run by the one and only headliner, YOU, let's get down to the nitty gritty good stuff.

But first, time for some real talk. I have found that I struggle with letting my emotions get the best of me and sometimes it prevents me from living the life I wish I was. Perhaps, you're also guilty of this. For instance, if someone upsets me, it seems to ruin my whole demeanor for the entire day, keeping me down and nothing gets accomplished. Like this book for example. I began writing it months ago and then things happening in my personal life affected me in such a way that I gave up on myself and my dreams. You know whose fault this all was though? MINE!

There's things that I have shared in this novel that I know without a doubt work, even if I'm not currently practicing them myself. It's all a part of the journey called life. Implementing new habits and replacing the old ones that don't work. Writing this book is also a form of self-care for myself. A reminder to do the things that are necessary for me to level up. So even as much as I'd love for you to take action on your life and do some of the things I have mentioned, I have written this is for me as well.

Get Out of Your Head and Into Your Life

"5, 4, 3, 2, 1", I counted to myself as I took a huge inhale in and exhaled slowly.

I had just finishing listening to The 5 Second Rule by Mel Robbins on Audible and decided I was going to start implementing this new tool into my life. Oh, and by the way, if you haven't yet checked out Mel's book, once you're finished reading this one, it's something you must change, immediately. No, I don't personally know Mel, we're not besties, although I do think that would be pretty freaking cool as she seems like a Superstar of a lady.

"Hey Mel, if you ever do happen to read this, it would be incredible to meet you someday. Perhaps, I can fly down and we can meet up for lunch and ogle some paintings. You never know, maybe I will be called to one."

I've been going through a very challenging time in my life. I mean we all have difficult times and what I find hard may not be exactly the same to you, but it's a mere competition game. Mentally and emotionally I had hit rock bottom. I've heard of people hitting there before but I never thought I'd ever see it and I can tell you for damn sure, it sucks.

I hit so hard that I was in disbelief that anyone truly cared for me. That I was unimportant. That I wouldn't be missed by anyone had I just decided to disappear. I knew internally that this was wrong but I just couldn't convince myself to believe otherwise.

"5, 4, 3, 2, 1. You matter. You are loved and you are important to many. You've inspired and motivated many people to change their lives. You are needed." I knew it, I just had to believe it. But how?

For many years I was one of those people who needed constant reassurance, for anything. If I was doing a good job. If someone liked or loved me. If I was missed. If I looked okay, amongst many other things. Sometimes, I still find myself craving this reassurance. I'd be lying if I said I had perfected it in any way.

Being reassured of certain things does makes you feel good, temporarily, but you shouldn't rely solely on them. Your opinion is the only one that matters. Sure, it can help boost your ego and build you up, but these are also things you need to learn to do yourself. You are in the game of life for yourself.

So by counting backwards, it changed my train of thought and I was able to focus on more important things. Also, when I paid closer attention to the actions of others and signs around me, I knew where I stood with others and how they felt towards me. I had in fact mattered to many. I had impacted many and I would be missed by many.

How did it change my life you ask? Well, essentially how it works is anytime a situation, thought or obstacle gets in your way, you count backwards from five and it reprograms and distracts you from the thought that crept in so you can refocus on what you really want or need to do. For example, make an important phone call, have that conversation you've been dreading, talk to your crush and so on. Any time you are hesitant on something, try it! It really works!

If you interrupt the thought within five seconds you'll easily be able to shift your focus to something else. Beyond the five seconds, you begin to get lost in those thoughts and they can take you down the wrong path, sinking deeper and deeper. Before long, you've wasted countless hours sitting in your thoughts and accomplishing nothing. Your goals, or whatever else you wanted to focus on, has begun to drift further and further away.

Once you have your thoughts under control, go focus on what you want to get done. If you're anything like me, you love creating lists. Sometimes I'll write down silly little things like *shower*, so I have something to cross off. You can even take it a step further and buy a fancy planner with an inspirational saying on the front and create a schedule. Time block out things you want to do throughout the day and stick with them. You'll be so busy, you won't have time to allow the thoughts to creep in. Write down ten things you'd really like to accomplish in the day, making the top five the most important, in case you don't make it further down the list.

Don't know what to write in your planner because you don't feel like you have these huge, audacious goals. Think about things that make you happy. Things you may have taken part in before kids or if you don't have kids, things that used to make you happy or wanted when you were younger. Maybe something you've previously done that you haven't in a long time. Like go to a concert or travel someplace, even local. Make a plan to save money and take the kids to Disneyland or a trip within a different city outside the one you live in. Connect with an old friend and have a coffee date. The options are endless.

I know covid hitting the world put a huge damper on things and placed a lot of us in a state of suck, we lacked fun in our lives. Mental health dropped to an all-time low and many of us felt lost and depressed. It was a major state of confusion. How safe was it really out there? I contacted covid twice myself and although it kicked me down and drained me of every last ounce of energy, I still faired out alright. Some however, didn't end up so lucky, so being cautious was key. Living in a bubble, on the other hand, was not something any of us were meant to do.

Life isn't made for us to stay in one place or instead of legs, we'd have roots. I remember hearing a quote like that somewhere before and it just made so much sense. That's not verbatim, but it was something like that. You get the drift. The point of it all is to live. That's what direction I'm trying to make with this book. So many of us don't live, we just do. We go along with the day to day that life takes us. Every day is the same for so many of us. Get up. Go to work. Come home. Eat Supper. Go to bed. Repeat. BORING!

Let's change that! Let's break the chain of mediocrity. We were made for greatness. We each have a purpose. Some of us know what that is, some of us haven't yet found it. I know mine is to make a difference in people's lives. To change their perspectives on how they view themselves and the world around them. To break them from their comfort zones and show them how they can do whatever their mind and heart desires. Like I said at the very beginning. You're the only one that can decide how your life will go. You're the only one that decides what to choose to deal with, how you react to certain situations and the boundaries you allow in their life.

I'm sure if you think about it right now, there are a few things you would change. Things you're allowing yourself to deal with that you really don't want to. It's all up to you on what you desire in your life. Welcome to my world. I understand my worth (now) and I know what I should and shouldn't accept and when to turn around and walk away. Being stuck in constant patterns and beliefs will make it harder to break through the norm. At least

I'm being honest. I hit roadblocks as well. Like I said, I'm alongside you for the journey. We're doing this thing called life, hand in hand, together.

That's where this book will become helpful for us all. It's like our own little book of wisdom, tidied up between the cover. Only reading the pages, won't typically alter anything. Actually taking action and implementing what is being suggested, may render some changes. It'll help with the creation of new habits and bidding farewell to the old ones. I really don't want you, any of you, to live a life of regrets. Time really does go way too fast. We all deserve to enjoy every moment of it. Loving every day. Being grateful for the good and bad that helps shape us into these beautiful people we were meant to be. It could take some time, but you will get there. So, will I.

So, what could potentially be standing in your way? Could it possibly be your mindset? Haven't yet incorporated good habits? Could it be a person, someone you love perhaps? Is it fear? Afraid of what others will think? Afraid of failure, or even maybe success? Afraid of change?

You're standing in your own way if:

1) **You aren't allowing yourself to fail.** Again and again. Success only comes after failure. Usually numerous times.
2) **You aren't surrounded by the right people.** Surround yourself with those whom are ahead of you and you can learn from. People who think BIG.
3) **Your BIG picture isn't BIG enough.** If what you're aiming for doesn't scare you, think BIGGER. Make it so big, it seems unrealistic to even reach.

4) **You're not resonating with your WHY.** Which is sort of like your big picture only the reason why you're after such a thing to begin with.
5) **You're too focused on the end result.** Enjoy the journey and all the small moments, mistakes, failures and learning curves along the way.
6) **You're afraid to ask for help.** From time to time, we all need help. Don't be afraid to ask for it. This doesn't make you less successful or less of a person, this actually builds on your character because you didn't allow your ego to get in the way.

So, to recap. Who's standing in your way? That's right, YOU! The one and only you.

Some amazing tools to get out of your head:

1) **Change the story you are telling yourself.** Even if you don't believe it at first. Repeat it as necessary until it becomes a belief installed inside you.
2) **Figure out what is standing in your way of your greatness.** Most times we already know what's holding us back, we just don't like to admit it. It could be a bad habit or belief we have created from childhood, regardless, it can be changed.
3) **Stop making excuses.** When we get in our head, we're simply making an excuse to not do what needs to be done, or think a thought that needs to be erased.
4) **Name the b!tch inside your head and tell them where to go.** Yup! Sounds simple but give it a try. It feels sooooo good!

CHAPTER TWO

Mindset Mastery

"Overthinking. The art of creating problems that weren't even there."

– Unknown

Tackle Overthinking

Say whatttttt?

Did you know that more times than not when you overthink something you are indeed creating new problems and ideas that weren't even there? True story.

Sometimes it's as easy as taking a step back and assessing the situation to see if there's any truth or proof to the new scenario or if your mind is simply just trying to protect you. The bitch certainly loves to do this on a daily basis. Protect from pain and bring us closer to pleasure, aka, our comfort zones, the familiar. Where dreams go to die.

I named mine. I recommend naming yours as well. Meet Esmeralda. It really helps that I can call her out on the hard days when she tries to get in my head. She's really bossy. It becomes much easier to tell her to take a hike, clearly a little more profoundly, now that she has a name. Try coming up with a full name to really get the full affect.

When you first read the quote at the beginning, did you by any chance overthink it? Question its truth? Are you denying the fact that you do create problems that weren't even there? I bet you stopped and thought about it for a minute. Hopefully, you went back in your mind and thought about a time or moment where overthinking may have come into play, to see if you could find the logic behind your reasoning. I know I did.

We're the worst at creating extra problems for ourselves that don't even exist, without even having the proof behind them. The problem you overthink about is rarely the issue. You create the problem by overthinking. Most of the harm is caused in your head and not so much from the actual outcome or situation. Hmmm...

I remember being pregnant. More so the first time than the second, but you hear all the stories of what could go wrong. Oh boy, overthinking when you're pregnant is never a good idea. Can you say hormones? Every little pain, ounce of discomfort, movement from inside, made me question if everything was going to turn out alright. My mind would feed me all sorts of made up beliefs. The baby is breached. The baby isn't breathing. Something's going to go horribly wrong during delivery.

I know some mommas have actually gone through this traumatic experience and I'm so very sorry if you're one of them. I can't even begin to imagine how horrible it would actually feel to live this. Just my mind feeding me the lies was painful enough. My deepest condolences to the heartbreak that would have followed.

Both of my pregnancies and deliveries ended up being problem free, and were quite easy, it was just me getting in my own head that made things more complicated. Proof that overthinking can cause issues that aren't even there.

Overthinking can also be the symptom of a deeper issue like stress, anxiety and depression. Dwelling on your mistakes, problems and shortcomings can increase your risk of mental health problems, as it causes it to deteriorate. It can create an unhappy life and rob you of joy and the things that matter most. It can also bring you further from your dreams and goals. Can you think back to a time you overthought about something and it ended up working out in the end or even better than you could have imagined?

Sometimes you just have to let things be and not react or think. You'll be more peaceful and content that way. One thought can ruin your entire day, most times it isn't even worth it. What it really comes down to is learning how to master your mind and keep control. Worrying actually creates more stress and problems than doing what needs to be done. It's so easy to over mentally exhaust yourself in the process. They say if you want to feed a problem, keep thinking about it. If you want to starve a problem, take action. A good percentage of problems are solved with less thinking and not more. With patience and a clear mind, you'll be able to focus more and find solutions.

Surprisingly however, not all overthinking is bad and damaging. Overthinkers can be more prepared for a situation, whether good or bad, because they've already played out all the possible scenarios. They sometimes appear to be more productive and can be better decision makers, especially when creating a plan of action that requires something to be completed within a certain time frame. We're going to focus more on getting away from overthinking, as it's a huge waste of time in general.

Tips to fight against overthinking:

1) Unlearn the patterns that brought on the overthinking and create new patterns.
2) Find a way to change the narrative that keeps playing in your head.
3) Always check the facts against your thoughts before accepting them. How much truth can you find? Your thoughts love to tell you stories that most of the time aren't true.
4) Remove any triggers that may be causing the overthinking.
5) Distract yourself. Find something you enjoy doing to distract the fact that you're lost in your thoughts.
6) Meditate. Always a great way to feel your thoughts and then push them away.
7) Journal. Keeping track of your thoughts and worries. Empty your brain. Rip out the page and burn it if you wish.
8) Exercise. Moving your body every day, even if it's only for a quick ten minute walk. It's so good for your mental health and helps you clear your head.
9) Do something nice for someone else. This is always a feel good thing.

10) Try the 5 second rule as mentioned in the previous chapter. Count backwards from 5 and move on to something else.
11) Breathe deeply. There are many breathing techniques you can practice to slow your heart rate down when your thoughts are working you up.
12) Recognize negative thinking and replace with positive thoughts. This one can be challenging and can take some practice. It really is helpful, once you master it.
13) Acknowledge your successes. Find a time you were successful at something you wanted to achieve before and use it as an example if that voice in your head, your Esmeralda, begins convincing you otherwise.

Limiting Beliefs

"I'm not interested in your limiting beliefs; I'm interested in what makes you limitless." – Brendon Burchard

I'm worthless. No one loves me. I'm good for nothing. I'm not smart enough. I'm just a waste of space. I will never be successful. I'll never amount to anything. I'm not a good person. I'm not supported. You're nothing special. I'm easily disposable. I'm too old. I'll never be happy. Perhaps you've mumbled a few of these to yourself a time or two OR something along the lines of. You know it isn't true but sometimes you can't help but believe it. Maybe someone had said one of these to you before and you built up this belief system around it. It could be possible you have simply mistaken the actions or words of said person(s). Sadly, I have spoken every single one of these to myself or have had them said to me.

One of the biggest lies I've told myself was that I would never be a writer. I've said it for *at least* eight consecutive years, if not more. "This is the year!" I would tell everyone. "I'm finally going to publish a book." It never happened. Another year gone by.

A few years in a row I wrote an entire manuscript and quit during the editing stages. Most times I got as far as a page or two and quit. I started to believe what I was telling myself was in fact true. I was never going to be a writer at this rate. I needed to stop quitting on myself, but how?

Here we are again. A new year. THIS IS THE YEAR, I just know it! No one is stopping me, not even myself. You know how I know all this? I asked for help and got myself a kick-ass mentor who sees my potential and refuses to give up on me or allows me to give up on myself. It's really happening this time!

I always knew deep inside I was meant to be an author. It's in my heart to inspire others and help them live their best lives. I am meant for more and so are you! Every once and a while, you just have to push everything aside and just go for it. See where the journey takes you. You never know. By not hesitating you could change your life for the better.

We all fight limited beliefs. We all believe at one point or another that we aren't capable of what it is we'd like to achieve in life. We all feel worthless. We all struggle with that voice in our heads. Isn't she a real bitch sometimes? Always directing you away from what it is that you truly want, trying to protect you and keep you safe. Sure. None of us truly like change, but we must welcome it. Especially if you're on the path of growth. Change is necessary and change is enviable. In fact, we've all experienced change at one point or another in our lives. It usually makes us uncomfortable and forces us out of our little comfy ones we had built. To live our best life, however, this is needed. We need to begin welcoming change and wishing for more of it.

Look deep inside yourself for a moment. What are the lies you've been feeding yourself? If you answered "nothing", check again. We've all talked badly about ourselves at one point or another. It's inevitable that you have.

First, let's unwrap what limiting beliefs actually are for those of you that are unsure.

Limiting beliefs: A series of lies or stories we tell ourselves, that we begin to believe.

The issue with these is that it holds us back from becoming who we're meant to be. We begin to believe them. They sit in your mind and come out from time to time, especially if you do something wrong, mess up or can't figure something out. You'll begin thinking, "Maybe so and so was right. I'm really not smart." Perhaps, the guy you liked began talking to someone else and ghosted you. Pain and words from previous relationships begin flowing back in. "Maybe they were right. I am nothing special."

Stop right now! Stop beating yourself up! I, myself am extremely guilty of listening to these beliefs. I know I'm not any of these things, even though the feelings creep in. I am smart. I will be successful. I will accomplish all the things and DAMN STRAIGHT I am special! And so are you! We're Limited Edition baby, don't you forget it. Yes, you will hear me reference this a couple of times throughout the book because I really want it to sink in. There's no one like you. Even if you're a twin, you both have your differences. There's only and ever will be one of you.

Like I said, rare and limited edition. You were waiting for the "baby" to follow weren't you?

If anyone has ever said anything horrible to you like that, they are a piece of work and you don't need or deserve that type of criticism or negativity in your life. I get it's difficult to avoid it sometimes. Especially if you're living in it or its surrounding you, whether it's at home, your workplace or even friends. You need to find a way to ignore or walk away when those people strike. They will continue to drain you of your power if you let them.

Some limiting beliefs have been instilled in us since childhood so they can be extremely hard to break through. They have been unconsciously created based on our interpretations of painful experiences from the past. The good news is, they don't dictate your future unless you decide to let them do so. If your belief isn't steering you in the direction you're aiming to go, time to change it.

I know, I know. Easier said than done. I hear what you're saying. "Well thanks Laura, for the awesome advice; I'm just supposed to change my beliefs. Look, I'm snapping my fingers and nothing is happening," Good one!

Now hold on a minute. It may not quite be that simple, but it's also not impossible. Let's practice some techniques and put them into action, so you know how to make the change. You may feel triggered when they begin to seep in, but let's begin building up some resilience, in hopes you remember what to do. It's a daily practice. It requires discipline. One day it will become a habit, but until then, this is what I want you to do.

Think of the last limiting belief you have told yourself. Maybe it was one of the ones I shared in the beginning. Chances are it was today you thought of this belief. You have it all in your head now? Okay, good, now what I want you to do is think the opposite belief. Put a positive spin on it and be specific.

Let me give you an example:

"I am too old to..." It's a classic one I'm sure we've all used at once point. For this example we'll say "begin a business."

Switching the belief would look something like this, "I am never too old to chase my dreams, or to begin a business. Vera Wang didn't begin designing wedding dresses until she was in her 40s. Julia Child wrote her first cookbook at age 50. I can begin anything at any age. There are no limits."

See the difference between those two statements? See the power in the second sentence? It immediately makes you want to go and begin that business doesn't it? If not, it damn sure should! Read it again and again. Program it internally. Feel the energy it provides.

Let's take a look at another example.

"I'm good for nothing." Yikes! That's a harsh one and I hope no one truly believes this about themselves. If I'm being honest however, I have. It's not a good feeling and really makes you feel very crappy inside.

Let's switch it up.

"I am an incredible mom or dad. My friends and family look up to me and love me very much. I have people who depend on me. I have been promoted at work." Keep giving yourself examples of a times you felt like you were something, like you were needed or belonged. Continue doing this every time a thought like this creeps in.

It can take some practice. The hardest part is catching it when it begins. Before you get too lost in depth of the belief. You want to notice it right away so you have time to debunk it before it takes control. Remember "where your focus goes, your energy flows."

Another practice to instill before putting the positive spin on your beliefs is to ask how true the statement is you're telling yourself. "Where are the facts supporting this?" Ask yourself questions. "Have I always felt this way, or when did it begin?" "Is there something that could have triggered this belief?" "Is this belief progressing me towards my goals or pulling me further away?" More or less, you're arguing against your own initial thinking, looking for the proof. In most cases, you'll find none.

Once a belief begins to take over, you may begin to notice numerous beliefs creeping in. They will consume you and bring you to a lower state where your focus will be non-existent. You'll become lazy and begin procrastinating. Worst of all, your dreams and goals go out the window because you become trapped within your beliefs. I don't want that for you and I know you don't want this for yourself neither. Hence, why you picked up this book. Looking for some direction on living your best life.

I hope you're finding useful what I've been sharing so far. There's so much more to unpack so let's recap what we've covered so far and continue on with the goods.

Steps to overcome limiting beliefs:

1) First identify them.
2) Challenge your belief. Where are the facts supporting said belief for it to be true?
3) Adopt a new belief by flipping the switch.
4) Repeat said new belief.

Overcome Doubt

"A mind troubled by doubt cannot focus on the course to victory." – Arthur Golden

Doubt can kick in unannounced. Unexpectedly. Whenever it feels like it really. It happened to me as I began to write this chapter. "I don't know much about doubt besides how to feel it, so where do I begin with writing a chapter on it?" I thought to myself, but here we are anyways. My belief in myself is stronger than my doubt. Of course, I had to train myself to get there and I'm here to teach you the things I know and have learned.

I've doubted myself on many, many occasions. We all have and it's a hard habit to kick and once you start that spiral downhill it can get out of hand. It's hard to rise back to the top where the positivity floats around with butterflies and rainbows. Or is it unicorns?

Doubt can go fuck itself and I wish it never existed. Anytime anything seems to be going right, that little asshole likes to shows up and ask, "Yeah, but are you sure?" Then I begin to second guess myself and try to come up with evidence behind my beliefs, which is usually shit my head just made up and doesn't prove the doubt is in fact correct. It's evident some doubt just tried to take over, due to all the profanity. I wasn't going to add it in, because doubt told me not to. But, I told myself I was going to be raw and real with you all, so that's what you'll get.

Are you beginning to notice a pattern here? All of these topics sort of run together and are all relatable. Doubt falls along the same lines as limiting beliefs. Lies we tell ourselves. Beliefs that have been instilled in us. Our mind has one job, to protect us. It wants to keep us safe and comfortable. Anything outside of that, it will make us second guess ourselves.

Doubt is the confidence killer. Holds us back from doing all the things we know we are fully capable of. It prevents us from succeeding and believing in ourselves. It will prohibit you from living the life you really want, the one you desire. The one you continuously dream about.

Self- doubt isn't something you are born with, it is learnt as you age. As children, we are full of confidence, but that changes overtime as our environments change or we're affected by the opinions of others.

When it comes to self-doubt there's more than one kind. Firstly, there's self-sabotage. We all are experts at this at one time or another. It blocks us from accomplishing our goals and reaching success. Something we know we don't want in life, that's why we're here, right?

Second comes imposter syndrome. This one used to hit me hard and still does occasionally. I question how I'm capable of helping someone live their best life, when I'm not currently doing it myself? It's when you feel like a fraud. I'm on my way though. I know the things that need to be done. Some things take a little more time to build up a habit.

The perfect way to sum up imposter syndrome was best pointed out by Mel Robbins, during one of her episodes of The Mel Robbins Podcast. I love Mel Robbins, if you couldn't already tell. She says to scrap the term imposter syndrome because when you're new to something you're a student. You clearly don't know everything in the very beginning. You're a beginner, you're not faking anything. You're actually figuring it out. It's part of the process you have to go through. I hope that makes you feel a little better.

I know it did for myself. Oh, the imposter syndrome that kicked in writing this book. I don't know what the hell I'm doing. I've never published a book before. Chances are, the first edition, what is being released, isn't going to be my best work. I'm sure there could have been a bazillion ways I could have made it better. But, I did it and nothing held me back. That has to count for something, right? I'm sure there's things you'd love to do but you're too afraid to do it because it's all new to you and you may suck at it. Oh well, we're all new in the beginning. Do it anyways!

The third kind of self-doubt is worrying that whatever path you choose will be wrong. This can cause you to struggle to make big or small decisions, in most cases making no decision at all.

Some tips to help with self-doubt:

1) **Journaling.** As mentioned a couple of times previously, this is a great way to get everything out.

2) **Seek professional help.** Sometimes it comes down to needing help from a professional if the doubt gets too out of hand. You should never be ashamed to seek help.
3) **Second guess your thoughts.** That's right, get skeptical. You are not your thoughts. Begin asking yourself questions on how accurate your thoughts actually are.
4) **Spend time with people who are supportive.** When you're surrounded by those that support and believe in you, you will then begin to take on that belief as well. Try to spend less amount of time with or avoid those who put you down. It's damaging to your mental health. Spend more time with those that make you feel good and build you up.
5) **Self-reflect on past achievements.** As mentioned before, find a time you have accomplished something. It reminds us that we are capable of what we want to achieve.
6) **Be nicer to yourself.** Practice self-compassion. Start saying nice things to yourself daily. Point out things you love about yourself.
7) **Don't play the compare game.** Comparing yourself to others will only make you doubt yourself more. Be thankful for what you have right now and be proud of working towards what you want. If you're trying to deny yourself that you're not working towards anything, you began by picking up this book looking for guidance. That's a step in the right direction. Everyone's life, skills, environments, likes, dislikes and strengths vary. You'll never win by comparing yourself to others.

Back in Control

"The only thing that's keeping you from getting what you want is the story you keep telling yourself." – Tony Robbins

So to summarize everything you just read, it's time to stop living in your head and get back in control of your life. Wouldn't you agree? Again, your mind is built to bring you closer to pleasure and further from pain. It's why it's always protecting you or presenting you with the worst case scenario. It wants to show you how much safer where you are is and how scary and dangerous the alternative could be. Sometimes, it will find ways to talk you out of the things you really want. There's umpteen amounts of science that backs this up but I'm not about to bore you with all the research findings. Go ahead, take a look. There's this thing called Google. Ha!

The reason it's so difficult to close this mindset part down is because I truly feel it is one of the most important things you need to master when it comes to living life. If you can't get past all the stuff in your head, you'll remain stuck there until you can. Your dreams and goals will pass you by. New love and opportunities, everything will. Time just keeps on ticking, it won't wait for you. It's all up to you on how you decide to use it. I spent way too much of my precious time upstairs, I don't want you to make the same mistake I did. So, get out of that pretty little head of yours and begin living your best freaking life, however that looks for you.

CHAPTER THREE

Your Why

"Find your WHY and you'll find your way."
– John C. Maxwell

Ever want something so badly, like it had a tug on your heart that you just couldn't shake? You just knew it was meant for you but you had no idea on how you'd obtain it. There's obstacles you have to face and challenges to overcome, but you feel like you'd cross a jungle full of poisonous and deadly creatures just to get to it. That! That is when you know you've found a strong enough why. A strong desire. Your calling.

Some people don't know their why. Why something calls to them. Perhaps you have the opposite going on. You want something, or think you do but continuously give up on going after it because you haven't given it a strong enough reason as to why you want it in the first place. Therefore, it's not as important to you as you may have originally thought. But, when it is, nothing will stand in your way.

The first step in determining your why is to think of something you want. For example, I always wanted to publish a book. Write this down in the middle of the page, sort of as if you're brainstorming. Draw lines coming off of that word in all directions and write down as many reasons you can think of, on why you want to achieve what you're going after. You may want to publish a book for the fame, or the money. Maybe it's the acceptance from others because you've always been looked at or felt like a failure. Perhaps, you're aiming for success or that pure sense of satisfaction of finally completing something you've been saying for years you were going to do. Maybe you're hoping to become a New York Times Bestseller and meet other famous authors.

All it can take sometimes is that first bad day and it throws everything off. How about a day you don't feel like doing the things you know you should be doing, so you can accomplish or obtain that thing you want? You'll need to go back and revamp your why if anything makes you want to stall. Regardless, whatever the reason, make sure, WHY you want to do it is so strong that nothing will keep you from going after it and keep you pushing forward.

If let's say someone you knew was dying from cancer or even had cancer, perhaps the reason you wanted to write a book was to take a good portion of the proceeds from sales and donate it to charity to help with more research and in help finding a cure. A cause that's near and dear to you. So you reasons could go a lot deeper than just becoming wealthy. Not that there's anything wrong with wanting to become wealthy. Wealth sometimes has a bad reputation but a lot of good can also come from it.

You can help out struggling family members. Get caught up on debt, pay off your house and car. Save more for retirement. Live comfortably. Not having to cross your fingers every time you use your bank card at a store, waiting to see if it will decline or not. I've been there, many times. Always checking the bank before you enter a store, making sure there is enough in there and calculating everything on your phone as you pick it up to make sure you don't go over that said amount. Letting a big sigh of relief out when it's approved. Whew! Another embarrassing moment avoided. Maybe you can relate?

Creating the drive to go after the things you want requires a lot of patience and discipline. Motivation plays a part in the whole scheme of things as well. You need to gain clarity on what you want and say no to anything that isn't it or the things that will deter you away from the direction in which you wish to head.

A clear why will help you focus your efforts on what matters the most to you. It can push you to take risks regardless of the obstacles in your path as I mentioned at the beginning of this chapter. Firstly, take a look at your strengths and what makes you come alive. You can use those to help break it down and find your purpose.

Do you know your why? Do you know the very thing that keeps you pushing forward, NO MATTER WHAT?

Let's unravel this for a minute.

1) What makes you come alive? Like really lights you up!
2) What inspires you?
3) Have any passions?
4) Recall what you used to like doing as a kid.

Why it's good to find your why and the benefits of knowing it.

1) **It will keep you laser focused on your goals.** When something is important to you, it's easier to stay committed.
2) **Helps with living longer.** Studies have shown when you live with a purpose, you look forward to everyday and it can lead to a longer life span.
3) **You develop a sense of resilience.** You learn to steer away from anything that is preventing you from achieving your goals.

Passions, Goals and Hobbies

"Don't ask yourself what the world needs – ask yourself what makes you come alive, and then go do it. Because what the world needs is people who have come alive." – Howard Thurman

Originally, I planned on writing different sections for each of these but like everything else I have mentioned in this book, it all sort of ties together. They are all equally important and play different roles in your life, without any of them, I feel like life isn't complete. Maybe you're completely happy not having any passions, goals or hobbies, but in my opinion, life would be pretty blah without them, I would think anyways.

Think back to when you were a small child, yet again, you had them all. You had things you were passionate about and loved doing. You had goals, things you wanted to accomplish, and you had hobbies. As we get older, some of us seem to condition ourselves. Society tells us who we should be and what's right or wrong. No problem, we just need to be reprogrammed. Listening only to ourselves and doing what we feel is right to do, is a great place to begin.

My biggest problem is I have too many passions, too many goals and too many hobbies. What I don't have is enough time to give to them all. Sometimes, I feel all over the place and I lose all sense of who I really am, what I'm called to do and my purpose.

I know and I feel it in my heart, that helping people live their best life is what I was called to do. People easily gravitate and open up to me. I give off that welcoming vibe, I've been told. There's never any judgement. I'm always as helpful as I can be and know the right things to say, apparently. If you need a good kick in the butt, well I've been told I'm good at that as well. Maybe it's because I can relate with a lot of them. We've been through similar pain and trauma. We feel lost and like we don't belong. You know what I've been learning though, that's okay to feel like you don't belong. We were made to stand out!

Here's some dirt on me. Some of my passions include writing (shocker), exercising and helping others live a healthy life, travelling to exotic places, being outside in nature, spending time with my family and friends. I love being surrounded by people and I also love time to myself.

Goals. Where do I begin? Obviously, to become a best-selling author. Continue writing books. I'm also a health and wellness coach and I'd love to grow my team and help as many women as I can. I want to rise to the top, create my own fitness app and begin creating my own programs. I've also wanted to create my own planner. I have goals of owning multiple companies and grossing over a hundred million a year. There's no limit to what your goals can be. Dream big!

You should never aim small. There's that satisfaction that comes with reaching a goal, but you have to enjoy the journey along the way and some people forget that. Guilty! I sometimes just crave that end result and don't enjoy all the things I had to go through to get there. The sweat and tears. Late nights and early mornings. When things get boring and are no longer fun. If you aim big, so big they feel unattainable and unrealistic, it will push you to greater lengths to get there. This can backfire with some people. They see their goal as too far into the future and give up. The trick is to make small, more attainable goals leading up to the big goals.

Reverse engineering your goals, if you have a timeline in place, will give you an idea on when you need to have certain things accomplished by. For example, let's say you want to write a 50,000 word book in a year. Yes, I seem to use writing a book for a lot of examples. It's simply what's fresh in my mind right now. To figure out what you'd have to write each month, you'd take the 50,000 total and divide it by 12 months. So, 4167 words a month. If you're trying to figure out how many a week you'd have to write, divide by 4 or 5, depending on how many weeks are in that month and so on. It sounds complicated but it's fairly simple to figure all that out.

Quick word of advice - keep your goals to yourself. Work in quiet for some time and then disclose of them when you're close to accomplishing them. It saves yourself from the embarrassment if it doesn't come into fruition and you won't have others trying to convince you that you are crazy. That you will never reach that obscene goal. Trying to discourage you to quit, sometimes it does work. You will have those that do support you and it's good to have a small accountability group to help push you forward, but for the most part, keep it to yourself. You're the only one that understands why your goals are your goals and it's not supposed to or will makes sense to anyone else. All they can provide you is their own opinion on why it's a good idea or not.

Hobbies. Does collecting things count as a hobby? I seem to do very well at collecting things. I collect coins. I know, so very random. I've been doing it since I was a young girl. It's about the only thing I really collect, besides journals I guess. I think I have about 8 of them and I started using each one. Key word – started. Writing. I do write for fun believe it or not. It's something I've always enjoyed.

At one point I apparently had quite the collection of slow cookers, roast pans and muffin tins. I really hate throwing anything away. If someone is getting rid of something, of course I will take that off your hands. I have since learned to say no. I only found out about this crazy collection when we were moving from one place to another and some friends of mine were helping me pack and managed to point out that I don't need 4 slow cookers, 7 roast pans, and 6 muffin tins. Maybe the numbers were more, I can't remember now, but it was more than the average person. I now only have 4 muffin tins (2 big, 2 mini), an Instant Pot (hello, all in one), and 3 roast pans (all different sizes). Go me!

I enjoy getting lost in a good book, whether it's in paper format or on Audible. I love cooking, 4 wheeling, boating, hiking, camping, learning new skills (I'm always enrolled in some kind of course), the list goes on and on. Like I said, way too many of each.

Let's dive in to see if we can help you unravel some of the things about you. First, let's unpack your passion or passions and no I'm not talking about the Soap Opera.

1) What are you passionate about? Pay attention to where you spend your time, focus and money.
2) Are there certain things you enjoy sharing with or teaching others?
3) Try different things. Expand your knowledge. Surround yourself in different environments. Eventually, something will spark your interest.

S.M.A.R.T goals. I'm sure you've heard the term somewhere before, I think by now a lot of us have. In case you haven't let me break it down for you. When making goals, make sure they fall under the SMART goal framework. The acronym SMART stands for:

Specific: Get very specific and clear on what your goal is. Use as much detail as you possibly can.

Measurable: What evidence will show your progress? How will you measure your success?

Attainable: Set realistic goals, for your smaller goals to help you achieve the bigger one. They must challenge you but are achievable.

Relevant: A goal that relates to your ambitions. How does this goal align with others?

Time-bound: The time frame for accomplishing a goal.

Weight loss always seems to be the easiest when giving examples of a SMART goal. It also seems to be what a lot of people desire these days. After the rounds of covid that have gone through the world, people getting depressed, losing jobs and unable to socialize, had made some people eat and sit a lot more than usual.

So goal: I want to lose weight.

S - I want to lose 50 lbs.

M - I will keep a tracker on the weight that is lost. I will take before and after pictures.

A - I will aim to lose 5 lbs a week until I reach the 50 lb weight loss goal.

R - I want to become healthier and have more energy. Losing weight will set me up on the right track to do this.

T - I want to complete this within 6 months or less.

As you can see, it's fairly simple to break it all down and this should make you want to go revisit some of the goals you have been wanting to accomplish and help you break them down into a more recognizable plan.

Hobbies are simply things you enjoy doing in your free time or enjoy doing period. I'm sure I don't need to go into greater detail about what a hobby is. If you don't feel like you currently have any hobbies, you just need to examine a little closer. Do you enjoy reading? Knitting? Doing yoga? All forms of hobbies. Think about some of the things you enjoy doing. What do you like?

Exercise, Meditation and All The Feels

It may appear a little random to go from hobbies, goals and passions to exercise and meditation but I had to throw it in there somewhere and this seems as good a place as any. What? You didn't find any humor in that? Meditate on it.

It's not simply because I do exercise almost daily that I find it important, I just know it's good for the health benefits and longevity. Energy levels rise, all your feel good hormones (dopamine, serotonin, endorphins and oxytocin) are way up there, helping with decreasing depression and anxiety. Once you've created the habit, you begin to feel better about yourself, you will begin to see results which increases your self-esteem and confidence. A sense of accomplishment sets in. It improves your mental health and reduces the risk of certain diseases. You improve you mobility and ability to do certain activities. It strengthens your bone and muscles and reduces stress. I just can't stress enough the importance of moving your body. Everyday. Even if that is only a ten minute walk. As you age, your mobility and joints weaken. Taking care of yourself, definitely helps with that. I just can't understand why someone wouldn't want all of that. It's like the total package!

Meditation, now that's something I wish I could get on board with. I've tried and I've tried. If you already do it, good for you, maybe you can give me some pointers. I have a very hard time sitting and just being with myself. The thoughts begin to flood in and take over my peace. Things that need to be done start to weigh on me. Being alone with my thoughts is not a good place for me. Typically sadness creeps in and I begin to think about all the people who's done me wrong and I try to understand why it happened. It creates pure confusion for me and I usually end up feeling much worse.

I've been told that if thoughts begin to creep in, to journal it all out or write it on a piece of paper to clear it from my mind, so I can just focus on stillness and my breathing. I've also been told to pretend you're pushing the thoughts away like they are little clouds every time they appear. I need to just let everything go or try to make it work and be okay with it. I don't want to miss out on something that could better my life, before life is over and it's too late to do something about it.

If you're someone like me who just can't meditate, here are some helpful steps I have found that I'm going to implement the next time I try.

1) Sit somewhere quiet and that feels calm to you.
2) Set a timer, if you wish. Maybe begin with a smaller time until you get a little more comfortable with it.
3) Pay attention to your breathing.
4) Focus on your body posture. Are you sitting up straight?
5) Make note when your mind has wandered. Take notes if you have to.
6) Be kind to yourself and your thoughts.
7) End it with kindness.

Let's for a moment, focus on the four feel good hormones and what each are known for and how you can boost them.

Dopamine – The Reward Chemical. You can feel a rush of dopamine after certain things such as completing a task, eating food, involving yourself in self-care activities, trying something new, checking something off your list or even listening to music.

Serotonin – The Mood Stabilizer. You can get a rush of Serotonin from exercise, soaking in the sun, meditating, running, walking in nature, swimming or any form of movement really.

Endorphins – The Pain Killer. You can get your endorphin high from dark chocolate, exercising, laughing, and creating music or some form of art.

Oxytocin – The Love Hormone. This one's fairly simple self-explanatory. Oxytocin hits when you hug someone you love, play with a baby, hang with friends, play with animals, hold a hand, give a compliment, show affection and doing something nice for someone..

If you want to feel on top of the world, try hitting all four of these daily. It will boost your mood intensely making you feel unstoppable to the world. Bringing you down will be out of the question.

CHAPTER FOUR

Leaving Your Comfort Zone and Facing Fear

"If you want something you've never had, you have to do something you've never done."

– Thomas Jefferson

You guys, I have had to leave my comfort zone. Many times in fact. Sometimes by choice, other times, not so much. Have you ever been called upon to speak in front of a class? I'm sure that familiar feeling in the pit of your stomach is coming back just from me mentioning it, isn't it? What about at a strip club? Yes, I said strip club.

I took acting in school from elementary all the way through high school hoping it would help me work through the fear of speaking in front of audiences, and not to mention the fact I was going to meet Leonardo DiCaprio someday. Needless to say, I didn't pursue a career in acting.

Fast forward a few years out of high school, things had just ended with my current boyfriend and one of my besties decided that perhaps we'd hit up the local strip club to get me away from moping about the apartment and get my mind off things. I mean hot, naked men dancing around to hit music at the time with water pouring down over top of them, where do I sign up? I was a little different in my early twenties.

Long story short they were doing a contest at the time on who could give the best BJ to a banana. Somehow I ended up being chosen to go up in front of the crowd along with a few other ladies. Problem being, I didn't hear what I was supposed to be doing. Being handed a banana at a strip club, you'd think it would be obvious. Apparently not to my close-minded brain at the time.

I was starving. I'm sure you can see where I'm headed with this. Yup, I was that girl! I took a big bite of that banana, right there in front of everyone. Now just imagine for a minute how the audience reacted to that one. I was already way out of my comfort zone for being up in front of everyone and then I go and add to the discomfort. Go me! Not that it matters, but I know you're all wondering if I ever returned after that. Of course I did! In fact, I wasn't forgotten after that one as you might imagine.

Besides fear, I was also struggling with my mindset and accomplishing big goals I had set for myself that I took the leap and decided to get myself a Life Coach. Angie is amazing by the way! I had learned over the course of a year that the best of the best have coaches, in fact, all coaches need coaches. Perhaps you need a business coach, life coach, health coach, whatever it is you are trying to succeed with, you will excel with a coach.

We learn from those more experienced and ahead of the game from us. I was having a huge down moment in life and my life coach, Angie, was able to work with me to come to a conclusion on what needed to be done to pull me out of this funk. It took facing fear to ask for help. It took stepping out of my comfort zone to even admit that I needed help. I was always the person to figure things out for myself and sometimes that meant going around in circles and accomplishing nothing. Yup, I needed help. I needed to stop being stubborn and make that move.

We all enjoy being comfortable. In fact, studies have shown that many people get to the end of their life, never riding out their dreams and goals they set for themselves because they fear the unknown. Did you know about 92% of people give up on their goals each year? 92%!! That's a lot of people staying in their comfort zones! They are comfortable, even if unhappy, it is what they are used to. No one particularly loves change but it is a requirement for growth.

Some people choose to stay in their comfort zones because they have a fear of failure or maybe they actually fear success. Thinking about how their life would change if they were successful. Would people be envious of them or think negatively about them? Others lack belief in themselves and what they are potentially capable of.

Lack of understanding how to set a goal, committing to the goal and inactivity are high on the reasons why many stay right where they are. There are many different ways to map out a goal plan but making it specific enough and attainable is key. Set dates on when you'd like to accomplish certain things. Some goals can be life changing, so setting up your mindset for those changes scares some people. Entering the unknown means facing your fears. Inaction is where goals go to die. Just start.

Having too many goals can also lead to incompletion. Hello, it's me! Your focus is everywhere. You're trying to accomplish all the things. You put a little bit of focus into each thing, ending with feeling overwhelm from accomplishing nothing. Totally me. I want to accomplish and succeed at so many things, I've always wanted to publish a book. This has been a goal of mine for probably close to twenty years now. Most years I'd start, then my focus would get turned onto something else. I completed a few manuscripts and then never continued to the editing and publication stages. Why? I guess doubt crept in. Caring too much what others would think and also having too many goals on the go at one time.

An ah-mazing book to check out that focuses all on facing your fears is *Fear Is My Homeboy* by Judi Holler. I love reading physical books but sometimes I don't always get a chance to do so. Lately I have been listening to books on Audible while I'm doing other things like dishes or folding laundry. I'm huge on working on my well-being and listening or reading books is a big part of that. I'm up to taking others advice and trying things that work. One of my favorite things I learned out of *Fear Is My Homeboy* is fear setting. We've all heard of goal setting but have you heard of fear setting? How genius is that?

If you have big goals you're afraid to work on or feel like you'll never reach, a fear set could be just the thing you're missing. Grab a piece of paper and across the top write your goal or dream. Then make five columns. The first column at the top you will put *Excuses for why you can't.* For the second column you will write *What could go wrong?* Third column *How would you recover?* Fourth *What's the cost of inaction?* Lastly, *What could go right?*

I know, right? How amazing is this? I immediately jumped on board with this once I learned it. What a difference I feel this will make. Breaking it down and seeing the cost of inaction it what really hit me hard. What it was costing me to not follow through on my goals and dreams was obviously the life I was dying to live.

In most cases what we fear is what we should be doing. Need to say something the scares you? Just say it. What's the worst case scenario if you don't or think about the best case scenario if you do! Most of us know in order to grow and become our best selves that we have to do the scary things. The things we're most afraid to do.

Ways to make leaving your comfort zone a little less painful:

1) **Try switching up your routine.** This may be difficult for some of you, but already making that change will encourage you to only make more when you see it isn't so bad after all.
2) **Take on a new skill or hobby.** Again, this could be hard for some of you to incorporate but it will open you up to a world of possibilities and new opportunities.
3) **Do something you've always wanted to do.** Okay, so this one may not make it less painful but what I'm trying to make you see here is by taking small, baby steps in a different direction, makes change that much more tolerable.

4) **Look at it in a different perspective.** You're leaving your comfort zone and entering your growth zone. Where you're uncomfortable is where you learn.

External Circumstances

"We cannot choose our external circumstances, but we can always choose how to respond to them." – Epictetus

One of the best things I had heard and I'm not even sure where I had heard it from or who had said it, but it was one of the best pieces of advice. "Someone else's opinion of you is none of your business." It was something along those lines anyways. I've learnt to fit that into my every day. I'm no longer afraid of what others think about me or about what I do. It's none of my business, simply put.

According to Forbes "As long as you allow other people to have a negative influence over the way you think, feel, and behave, you'll struggle to reach your greatest potential. Giving away your power robs you of mental strength and derails you from your goals." Think about it for a moment, back to a time when you remember someone having such an influence over you whether it was positive or negative and how it impacted you and made you feel.

When someone positively has power over you, you live on this incredible out of this world high, but because you're reliant on them for this feeling, if they decide to take it away, you crash and burn hard, bringing you down feeling the exact opposite. Feeling buried.

If someone impacts you negatively, now we're talking an entirely different feeling. It's worse if it's someone you care about and had put trust in. If all you're hearing is harsh words and feeling negative energy surrounding this person you will begin to feel shitty about yourself and feel down, all the time. Depression and anxiety can kick in at an all-time high. Your goals and dreams? What are those?

It's your choice if you choose to let them control you or you choose to ignore them. You have to try not to let anyone suck the soul out of you and rob you of your power.

It can be increasing difficult to build up some resistance against what others may say and how they treat you, especially if they are still someone actively in your life. Some may try to break you down but you can't let them, whatever you do. It will deter you from the life you want. This is why it's good to build up a resilience against them and how they decide to be towards you. Remember, as I had previously mentioned, you can't control how someone will act, you can only control how you respond to it. You can choose to allow it to affect you or walk away because you're happy enough in your own power.

Your inner peace is one of the most fragile parts of you that you must protect. Once you allow someone else entry, it can destroy you and you will lose full control over yourself. This isn't always the easiest to do, but that's okay, I got your back.

How to protect your inner peace:

1) **Pay attention to your triggers.** We can usually figure out over time what those are and can sense when they are arising.
2) **Reduce your contact with negative people or say "sayonara" to them.** We all know who those people are in our lives whether we like to admit it or not. Some people I

understand you can't say goodbye to entirely because they could be a parent or a child, but maybe limit your time spent with them or point out how they make you feel and assist in helping them or getting them help. Sometimes there's an underlying reason as to why they are this way.

3) **Limit your social media and news consumption.** There's a lot of negativity in the news and online. Try to limit yourself on how much you engage daily. Even if social media appears to be more positive you may find yourself beginning to play the comparison game, creating the negativity within yourself.
4) **More importantly, don't forget to make time for yourself.** This is so very important and many miss this step, especially when they are constantly drawn to taking care of others. Well, you're someone too!

Protecting your inner peace is so extremely important and it took me most of my life, so far, to figure this out. It means protecting and caring about your mental, physical, emotional and spiritual well-being. This can look like setting boundaries for yourself, which we should all do. It helps us stay focused and make more clear decisions in our own best interests.

"Don't let the behavior of others destroy your inner peace." – Dalai Lama

Setting Boundaries

Some of us intentionally set boundaries but can quickly lose ourselves in relationships, friendships, obligations, careers or services we do for others forgetting why we set them in the first place. By breaking our boundaries it allows us to be taken advantage of and walked all over.

Good boundaries allow you to live a more peaceful life, living on your terms and figuring out what works best for you and your well-being. It helps you to decide what to say "yes" and "no" to.

Setting boundaries doesn't have to be something to overcomplicate. It's fairly simple to set them, it's much harder to stick with them, especially if you're a people pleaser or have a hard time telling others no. If you're constantly feeling burnt out, overwhelmed, tired of living your life for others, made too many commitments, loss of energy and your mental health has taken a turn for the worst, you could be overstepping the boundaries you have placed for yourself, or you haven't yet made any.

To live an intentionally good life, setting boundaries is a must. Boundaries for your partner, friends, work and yourself. Those who set healthy boundaries prioritize time for themselves and aren't afraid to say "no" if something will deplete them of their energy. They have higher self-esteem and respect for themselves. They have an extremely strong sense of direction and identity. They have no problem communicating their needs and what they are willing to tolerate. They rarely overcommit and are able to prevent themselves from being taken advantage of.

I've only just begun to take advantage of my boundaries. I was always a people pleaser and hated letting others down, leaving me depleted of energy, feeling stressed out and depressed. I allowed myself to be taken advantage of and let myself be used, even if it was hurting me. I was craving the attention, even if it was negative, even if it left me heart-broken. One day, I decided enough was enough. I know my worth, I know my value and it's something we all need to learn. We're worth more than the crap we allow to be okay with in life.

It is not okay, or normal, for someone to degrade you and call you names. It is not okay to allow yourself to be put down and be told you're good for nothing, even if you're the one saying these things. IT'S NOT OKAY! You need to set boundaries against what you will allow and not allow, especially with yourself. We're our own worst critics. I'm sure you already know that for yourself.

It's not okay to allow someone to use you for favors, you're better than that. If someone has treated you horribly and left you feeling heartbroken, sad, angry or confused, you're allowed to not let them back in your life. You deserve more than that. Don't be available for them because they are lonely. If they so easily disposed of you without a second thought, they aren't worthy of your time and energy. This is where your boundaries of what you will and won't tolerate come into play. Only make time for those who you know you truly matter to. The rest… fuck 'em. They shouldn't have taken advantage of you when you were around.

We're trying to work away from setting unhealthy boundaries. Being taken advantage of, giving too much of your time to other people, especially those that aren't deserving of it, have lower self-esteem and feeling overwhelmed by commitments you've made are signs of unhealthy or no boundaries. If you have a hard time saying "no" to others, you sometimes take on other people's problems as your own, or change yourself to fit in, it's time to make some boundaries.

To live your best life, you have to be at you best and that means a number of things. Setting boundaries tops the list, especially if you have big goals you want to reach, then setting healthy boundaries will get you there. You need uninterrupted time to focus and that means saying no to a lot of things sometimes, like outings with your friends. Going drinking at a bar until 3am is not going to land you that next client. Saying no thanks, will bring you closer to that.

Homework: I want you to begin saying no to things or people that drain you of energy. Start with one a week. We all know what they are for us. We all have those people who when we see their name pop up in a text or a call that we immediately feel that "drained energy" even without knowing what they want. You know, those people that you only hear of when they want something but they never seem to offer their help, even though they know you could really use it. And of course, you're not the type of person to ask.

Here's 5 quick tips in helping you set healthy boundaries:

1) Don't be afraid to say "no" to anything and anyone that will distract you from your time, deplete you of your energy and things that don't serve you.
2) Openly communicate the boundaries you have set for yourself with others.
3) Always take time for yourself.
4) Specify what your limits are and what you will allow.
5) When needed, remind others of your boundaries and if they are crossing them.

Adhering to the above will aid you in living a well-balanced life on the path to greater things. If this is a new thing to you that you're to implement, look at it as you "revamped". The new and improved you.

CHAPTER FIVE

Learn to Validate Yourself

"Your self-worth is determined by you. You don't have to depend on someone telling you who you are."

– Beyoncé

Beyoncé said it best. No one needs to tell you who you are or who you can be, that's all validated by yourself. It's entirely your decision. Nor should you depend on someone else telling you who to be. No one know what's best for you, than YOU. Remember back to the very first chapter, it's all up to who? That's right YOU. Who decides how their life is going to go? YOU! And who decides on what shit they will and will not tolerate? Again, YOU!

So, why is it important to validate yourself? Well, we're really good at doing it to others but many of us don't think to do it to ourselves. It seems we'd rather downgrade ourselves. The things we say to ourselves we wouldn't dare say to our best friend or someone we love so why do we feel it's okay to say it.

To begin validating yourself, even if it feels weird in the beginning, tell yourself how much you like yourself. Validating that it's normal to feel this way, and how proud you are of yourself. Tell yourself that you are safe and loved. You very much matter and you are worthy. You are more than your accomplishments and failures. That's a really good one. Sometimes we feel that's all we're good for and it's highly not the case. Other people's opinions are none of my business and don't determine my self-worth. It's all good to acknowledge that everyone makes mistakes. It's not only me.

I have an extremely hard time validating myself, it's something I constantly work on. While writing this novel, I've thought many times about scraping the entire thing and starting over. Had myself convinced that it was boring, no one would read it and it wouldn't be helpful to others. I felt it needed more stories and relatable content instead of "if you feel this, than try this content", even if what I was sharing would actually work. I told myself to just get through the writing part and when it came to edits, I can make the corrections where I felt needed.

I do have what it takes to be a best-selling author, I will change lives and people will read my book. This is something I tell myself repeatedly, even though I have a hard time believing it. Sometimes we have to lie to ourselves until it becomes believable. Our worth is not determined by our successes but our self-validation increases when we accomplish things that have been on our heart and mind. I don't need to publish a book to validate myself but how it will make me feel to finally complete something I've been wanting to do for over 20 years, is unexplainable.

People struggle with self-validation when they have little belief in themselves and what they are capable of accomplishing. I think most people have a problem with this at one point or another in their lives. This is where some turn to the validation of others to find their worth. This is a huge mistake because the only permanent validation you will receive is from yourself. Others aren't always going to see things your way or understand why you do things a certain way and this can change how you view yourself. Only rely on internal validation. Your opinion is the only one that matters.

Be easy on yourself and learn some ways to self-validate:

1) Accept all your flaws, mistakes and any limitations you may have. We all have these and it doesn't make us any less important than someone else.
2) Talk to yourself nicely and point out things you love about yourself.
3) Your needs are important, don't forget to prioritize them.
4) Acknowledge your efforts, successes, accomplishments, progress and any strengths you possess.
5) Encourage yourself, especially when the going gets tough. You got this!

Know Your Worth

"Sometimes the hardest part of the journey is believing you're worthy of the trip." – Glenn Beck

Never underestimate yourself. So many of us are guilty of this in many ways. One of the times I underestimated myself was with getting my license. I got them much later in life than most because I was always scared to drive. Well, that's what I always told myself anyways. I think they truth was I didn't believe it was something I could do. I was very good at talking myself out of things. "You're too scared." "You'll never be a good driver." "What if you die?" "You're not good enough." Yes, I talked to myself in a very sick way.

It took multiple tries to build up some form of belief within myself and resistance against the voices in my head to get behind the wheel. I didn't understand my worth. I didn't believe I was good enough or was going to be able to do it. Each time I was about to practice driving, I'd talk myself out of going, which resulted in another year passing by and another time I had to re-write my test.

I did finally get them, after failing the first road test, again because I allowed how I felt about myself to get in the way. I had myself convinced I was going to fail before I even did, and it happened. That only made things worse. It had only convinced me even more of the belief I already fed myself. I wasn't worth having the same privilege as everyone and was always going to be dependent on others.

Wrong! Was I so very wrong! Once I passed after my second try, everything changed. "I can do this." "I am capable of doing hard things." "I am just as worthy as everyone else." Something as silly as that, something most people do when they are sixteen, made me feel unstoppable. I immediately questioned other things I wanted to do and accomplish in life. So, I went and got my first tattoo. Wasn't nearly as bad as I thought it was going to be. Now, I'm writing a book that I'm going to publish. It isn't going to sit on my computer as this large .docx file that will never be touched. I'm going all the way! What comes next for me? Well, that's still up in the air, but I'm sure it'll be something grand. Something

I've always been afraid of doing. I have hundreds of things I'd like to do in life. These couple of things only opened the doorway and my eyes to what I'm capable of.

Can you think of a time that you questioned your self-worth and then you did something that made you feel on top of the world and you wonder why you ever doubted yourself to begin with? I'm sure you can think of quite a few times or situations. I feel once you get that taste of self-worth it makes you harder to break down. Oh, you still have days you will break, but it's so much easier to pull yourself out. Especially if you remind yourself of a time when you did something you never imagined you could do. It's a good practice to begin. We're all very worthy of living our best lives whether we believe it ourselves or not or if others try to convince us otherwise.

I came across a quote the other day by Eleanor Roosevelt, "No one can make you inferior without your consent." Ouch! It made me realize how much of my consent I was freely handing out. There was many a times I had felt inferior at the expense of someone else. What a stupid decision! If you're guilty of doing the same, I hope you decide to change that. Giving someone that much power over you is not how anyone deserves to soar through life.

Doing some deep soul searching had woke me up and made me realize some of the shit I was allowing in my life. People were hurting me, using me and walking all over me and I was allowing it. Why was I allowing it? It was only destroying me and my self-worth in the process. Shame on me!

I have some people in my life that I shouldn't allow to be a part of it and there's some people who have removed themselves that I wasn't ready to say good bye to yet. Though throughout all of the pain, confusion and resentment, there's lessons. Lessons I had to learn.

Lessons that woke me up to what I was allowing. I was blinded by whom they wanted me to see them as, not who they truly were. I believe they are all experiencing a sense of confusion on who their true selves are and I hope they all find peace within themselves to be better people.

Make Self-Love a Priority

How many hours a day are you making yourself a priority? Yes, I said hours. You should be making time for you. EVERY. SINGLE. DAY. You can't be present and at your best to help take care of others unless you first take care of yourself. This is especially important if you are a parent or responsible for taking care of your elderly parents.

There's a broad range of activities you can partake in as a form of self-care, whether that's grabbing lunch with a friend, exercising or getting your hair done. It looks so very different to us all. Essentially, it's something you do to progress your own mental, physical and emotional health. Engaging in self-care is vital to your health and helps us build resilience against the stressors we face in life. It leaves you better equipped to tackle even the hardest of challenges.

Self-care wasn't something I always practiced. In fact, it was only a couple of years ago I really began to dive deep into it. I used to get caught up way too much in the projection of social media. I wanted what others had. I was jealous and envious, little did I know, most people only show a reflection of their highlight reel and some people had to work really hard to get there. Some had endured and survived traumatic experiences, which I hadn't known until I began connecting with some of them. Some lost everything in divorces and separations and had to rebuild from the bottom. I began to admire their sense of identity, their power. Something they had that I did not possess was self-care. Even through all the hardship they had to find themselves amongst the rubble and fight through. They had to learn healing practices and ways to take care for themselves so they didn't crumble against the pressure.

I began to crack under the pressure with finishing this novel on time and getting it edited before launch date, which at the time while writing this is 3 weeks from today to be exact. With leaving everything down to the wire and last minute really started took a toll on me. I started doubting myself if I could do this and if I'd be ready. I then took a deep breath and exhaled. I was meant for this and I could do this. Anything was possible, I'd just have to work a little harder. I reflected back to some of the tips I have been sharing in the novel and took them into account. I went and did a thirty minute workout with weights and then got right to it.

Sometimes, even those of us that know better, simply need a reminder. None of us are perfect. We're all human and we all have different experiences, circumstances and situations that affect us and our wellbeing. I don't have any time for anything right now, except writing. That's where all my focus needs to go at this present moment.

Another important thing to remember is that our future self is not our past. We can't waste time thinking about what was, why things happened or how they are going. All we have is here and now and what we choose to do with that. The way we show up and the attitude that we bring daily will be reflected on how the day progresses. Time is never promised; we don't realize how lucky we are that we get to choose how we show up for ourselves. How are you going to begin showing up for yourself?

I've seen it mentioned somewhere before that self-love actually comprises of four different components. Self-worth, self-awareness, self-care and self-esteem. In order to have complete self-love you need to feed all four aspects. They are all fairly self-explanatory (like how I threw that in there), so no need to go into further detail on the each of them. I'm sure you know the things you can do to increase each one.

CHAPTER SIX

Overcome Fear of Failure

"Everything you want, is on the other side of fear."
– Jack Canfield

So many of us have things in our lives that we'd love to accomplish. Some even die with the successes they were hoping to achieve. Fear of failure can hold many of us back. Worried about putting ourselves out there and not being successful. Worried about how others will perceive us if what we said we were going to do, didn't actually happen. But, you know what? None of that matters. If say, whatever you're working towards didn't turn out as planned, well, all you found was one way it wasn't going to work. Try again!

It's not failure unless you give up, and I know that's not you. You wouldn't be reading this book unless you were looking for more in your life. If we were sitting across the table from one another sipping piña coladas, I'd be asking you to reassess the situation. Is there something you could have done differently to create the desired outcome? What is it about failure that you're afraid of?

Did you know that it has been said that it took Thomas Edison 10,000 failed attempts at creating the lightbulb? 10,000!!! How many of you can say you tried something that many times until it worked? I know I most certainly can't. When Edison was asked about all the attempts he simply said he did not fail but instead found 10,000 ways that won't work. Mic drop! We could all learn a thing or two from him!

I became a health and wellness coach back in 2016. In the beginning I had no interest at all in coaching others, I just wanted to embark on my own fitness journey, learning a thing or two along the way. Once I really got into it, I felt that I could indeed help others and be their own personal cheerleader as they began their own trek. However, the fear of failing began taking over. What if I wasn't good enough? What do I know that could possibly help them? I'm only new, no one is going to listen to me. I was so afraid of failing, that it was on my mind the entire time, and guess what? I failed to get my coaching business off the ground! I focused too much on what could go wrong instead of what could go right that the inevitable happened. Of course over time, I had to assess what I was doing wrong, learn from it and try again. Now, I have grown a strong team from not giving up and not being afraid to fail. With that being said, I'm planning on taking my cheer squad to the top!! That's how it's done, Queen! (and King!)

How to overcome fear of failure:

1) **Try, try, try again.** Yup, I said it. To overcome your fear of failure. Try again. Fail again and again, until it works. Soon you'll be so used to finding ways that won't work, you won't be afraid to fail. Especially in knowing that each time you do, you're getting that much closer to success.
2) **Block out the naysayers.** There will always be at least one person who doesn't agree with what you're doing or won't understand it. You're best way to avoid it is to ignore them and continue on with what you've been doing. Surprise them down the road with your success from not giving up.
3) **Look for examples of those who have had success from failure.** It's all around us if you just take a moment and look for it. There's been thousands of people who decided they weren't going to give up when they failed the first, second or third time. Eventually, things will work out if you stay consistent.
4) **Stop worrying about the outcome.** So many of us get caught up in the desired outcome. Worrying about how things will turn out can get you caught up in the moment and lose focus. Things may or may not work out. If you feel they won't work out, chances are, they won't. Once you bring your emotions into the mix, you begin to pay more attention to how you feel instead of being intentional.
5) **Remind yourself of a time you were brave.** Think of a time you overcame fear of failing. If you take the time to look around, I'm sure you can think of many scenarios. Most probably turned out better than you had imagined they would.

Laugh in the face of fear. I'm sure you can also think of a time you have overcome fear without even thinking about it. Maybe you were afraid to get on an airplane for the first time. Perhaps you were nervous to ask out your crush with the fear of being rejected. How about applying for that job you didn't have all the qualifications for? Maybe you were afraid of driving like myself. Whatever it was, there was something or many things you have overcome that you were first afraid to do.

When you think back throughout your life, you'll find many examples of times you were faced with fear but had overcome it and then questioned why you were ever afraid in the first place because it really wasn't that bad after all. Your first job. Meeting the parents of your first serious relationship. Moving and starting over. Beginning a new school. Maybe you were even afraid to sit on Santa's knee for the first time. The lesson I'm trying to make here is that after you get through fear, you'll have growth. You can and will survive. Maybe a little uncomfortably for a bit, but you will.

As mentioned above when I previously talked about fear, it appears to be one of the top reasons why many people fail to live their best lives. Fear of something. Fear of failing, fear of success, fear what others will think, fear of losing people, fear of change and a bazillion other fears that people face in this life. You must laugh in the face of them all, pull up your big girl or big boy panties, swallow your pride and get your shit together. Let's begin living this amazing life you so very long for.

Stop existing, Start living

Many of us walk around every day, doing the same routine. Get up, go to work, come home, eat supper, watch a little TV maybe and then off to bed. Yawn! Where's the excitement in that? You're truly just existing, that's it. Now, don't get me wrong, I understand some of you have jobs, kids and other obligations that may take up a lot of your time that you don't feel like you have a whole lot left by the end of the day. You have schedules you have to adhere to. I completely understand, I've been there too. If you wake up every day though and you're not looking forward to being awake or you're dreading another day, it's merely a sign you're only existing in your life. You need to give yourself SOMETHING to look forward to each day. Something that makes you jump out of bed in the mornings.

Throughout the past couple of years, maybe even longer, I have come across more and more people who were unhappy with their current status quo, but refused to do anything to change it. Myself, being one of these people. I'd often find myself complaining about things I didn't like or the way certain people were treating me but I didn't set boundaries nor did I make any changes, instead I decided to stick with the predictable.

Some people are afraid if they make certain changes that they could end up in a situation worse than the one they were currently in. They are willing to settle for a boring, predictable life over the chance of a possible successful and happy one. Now, it's not a guaranteed outcome of course, on the other side but how will you know, if you don't at least try.

Deciding to change your life for the better and break free from the norm is only the beginning. Making the change requires constant effort and hard work. Depending on the size of your goal depends on the amount of work it will require to reach. The harder the work, the easier it is to quit and resort back to your cookie cutter life.

If you ever think about giving up, it's important to remind yourself why you chose this direction in the first place. YOUR WHY. Remembering all that was wrong with the previous chapter of your life will help keep you heading in the right direction. Why does this goal so strongly resonate with you? Why must you accomplish it? Why is it important to you that you don't live a normal, comfortable life? What is it about your life that makes you unhappy? Are you really unhappy or just comfortable and craving some excitement?

All great questions to ask yourself when you're trying to figure out the next chapter of your life. Most importantly of all, don't forget to enjoy life on the way of figuring it all out. Savour each and every moment, they don't always last as long as you'd wish they had. Appreciate all the lessons you learn as they help you with growth. Too many people choose to exist over living since it's the easier option of the two. Instead, have fun pursuing your dreams. It sure as hell beats hesitantly waiting for life to pass you by.

Time to get your butt up off the couch and begin living that life you want to. Here's how:

1) **NO MORE WAITING.** Time is your most valuable asset. You need to live your life NOW. Every day that passes by is a missed opportunity and a day you'll never get back. Make every single one a good one! Stop waiting

around for amazing things to happen and begin making amazing things happen.

2) **Your health should be a top priority.** You'll hear me say this numerous times but it is extremely important. Maybe even more important that you'd like to believe. Good health is the foundation of a good life. It clears up the brain fog allowing you to focus more clearly on the life you're working hard for. You'll have more energy and feel better, leading to happiness. We all know where happiness leads.
3) **Figure out your purpose and say no to anything that isn't it.** Hustle hard for what you want and limit your distractions.
4) **Give more.** Whatever it is that you can give. Your time, materialistic items or maybe money. Ever notice how good you feel when you're able to give or help?
5) **Learn to say no.** As mentioned previously, you'll feel more at peace if you say no to the things you really don't want to do or the things that aren't projected on the path you're following. If you're anything like me you feel bad saying no, but sometimes you just have to. You'll feel bad for a short amount of time but if you had said yes, you'll feel completely drug out the entire time. Why put yourself through that?
6) **Have a bucket list?** Start crossing items off it!! If you don't yet have one, make one! Make a list of all the things you want to accomplish in life and check them off, one after another as you complete them.
7) **Stop wasting your life.** Whether that's on people, jobs or your thoughts. Enough is enough. Life's too short and your time is too precious. Only those that are deserving of your time and energy should get it.

8) **Embrace change.** Change is inevitable. It's going to happen at one point or another, whether we like it or not. Change can be very uncomfortable for lots but we must learn to welcome it and live with it.
9) **Spend more physical time with those that matter to you.** Less time on your phone and more in person conversations and quality time.

Sometimes it's so easy to get caught up in the busyness of life that we forget that this is the only life we get. We only get once crack at this. ONE TIME. That's it. Once it's over, it's over. This. Is. It. LIVE NOW!

Be Authentically/Unapologetically You

No one knows you better than you know yourself. There's also only one of you, so why would you want to be anyone else but you? Be proud to be you. Be proud to be unique. Be proud to stand out. Sure, there's things you'd love to change about yourself, we all have those. But, never wish to be someone else besides you.

If I have learned anything over the years it's to always be yourself. I have learned this the hard way unfortunately and had lost my true self for many years. I was someone that I was not. I catered to everyone else's needs and wants and I was unhappy. There's no worse feeling than being unhappy and just settling in your life.

There's nothing wrong with admiring certain qualities about someone, maybe the color of their hair, the way they carry themselves and so on but try to find ways that you can become a better version of yourself, and focus less on what the others have over you. Life isn't a comparison game.

Growing up I always envied those that had boobs. I have boobs, I'm just a little smaller chested then most. I always felt uncomfortable not having much and always wanted more. Tops seemed more loosely fit and I felt out of place. If I'm being honest, the thought of getting implants at one time, crossed my mind.

Now, at the ripe age of 40, I'm glad they didn't get much bigger. I've never had back problems. Guys never liked me only for my boobs and they are still perky and where they are supposed to be. Guess there was a silver lining after all. Tops these days seem to be made smaller, so it worked in my favour and I don't have to wear a bra if I really don't want to. It's a win – win! I learned overtime to love my true self, even the parts of me I wished I could change.

I always knew I was made for more. I had goals and dreams that I had put on the back burner because they didn't coincide with my current state of life or whom the person I was dating at the time. I lost me. I lost who I was. And who I wanted to be. I always had a burning desire inside me to reach for the stars and accomplish all that I could. But something always felt off.

I lost my desire to push myself. I lost the desire to be more. So I chose to settle and live the life I was dealt. The one I did choose but wasn't happy being a part of. I'm sure many of you have felt that way at times once or twice. It's not a good feeling by any means.

They say you become a product of who you surround yourself with. If you surround yourself with negative, unmotivated people, you will become one yourself. They also say if you are the smartest of the 5 people you surround yourself with the most, you need to find new people to be around. Ones that will motivate you and push you to grow. Ones that will encourage you to go after everything you desire. Are you the smartest of your bunch?

I noticed I was. It was a wake-up call. I loved the people I was surrounded with but I felt that they held me back from being something great. Sure, your own determination should be enough and you shouldn't require anyone's approval to do what you want to do. Yet, sometimes the encouragement and support is great to have. Someone to push you to be your best.

No one likes to surround themselves with fake people and if you put this front on for a while, eventually the REAL you will show its face. Do you want to face the embarrassment of someone finding out you were pretending to be someone you were not all along, or would you rather be truthful from the very beginning, flaws and all.

Sure, there has been times we all wish we were someone else. Lived their life, looked like them, idolized the stuff they had or things that they did, but that's no way to live. There's only one of you. There's ever only going to be one of you so you need to appreciate who you are, even if there's things you'd like to change. Some things you can, some things you can't. I like to look at us all as if we're all limited edition, because that's exactly what we are.

Not one of us is perfect, so if you believe otherwise, it's time to change that perspective. We all have flaws. We all have things that we don't like about ourselves. This is where confidence comes in and you love who you are anyways and be happy with the person you have become. Even celebrities wish they could change things about themselves as crazy as that may seem. We're all human and I think sometimes we tend to forget that.

Ways to win at being your authentic self:

1) **Take inventory of your life.** Are there parts of your life or people that are toxic? How about make you unhappy, resentful or angry? Make note of situations, activities and people that make you feel the most alive. Surround yourself more with those and less with the toxicity. Do you know when you feel the most authentic?
2) **Think back to who you were before you were in that relationship or surrounded by your group of friends.** What kind of goals and dreams did you have and why did you stop pursuing them? Go back to that person.
3) **Make a list of things you used to enjoy, things that made you happy.** Things that made life worth living. Think back to some of your joyous moments and best memories, what we're you doing? Who were you with? Why did you stop doing the things you enjoyed? Who influenced you to make these changes? What important role do they play in your life or are they perhaps just holding you back?
4) **Be happy just being you.** Learn to be happy with who you are in your limited edition body. Learn to change the things that don't make you happy or learn to deal with them. That is completely in your hands.
5) **If you're someone who's currently in the dating scene, show up on the first date as yourself.** Sometimes we want to impress our date, well usually most parties do. We try to be someone we are not in hoping we attract them to us. We pretend to be whom we think they want us to be.

This is the wrong approach. We think first impressions count and matter most, when just being yourself is what's going to seal the deal. Being your true self is going to help you in the long run.

CHAPTER SEVEN

Add in Joy. Feel Happiness

"Joy is the evidence of inner growth."
– Maria Montessori

You know, I began writing this novel and thought I had compiled all the perfect pieces of advice one would need to live their best life and then it dawned on me. One needs joy in their life for it to feel complete. How could I write a novel and not have a chapter about joy, how to find joy and bring it in to your life each day? It's such an important piece of the puzzle!

Without joy, there's no happiness. Without happiness, you feel no urgency to live and do the things you wish to do. We can't have that! This chapter is a must! Sometimes it means taking a step back and analyzing what's in front of you to find what's missing.

So joy, what is it exactly? We all think we know what it is but let's begin by diving a little deeper shall we. A lot of people seem to confuse joy with happiness and although they share similar characteristics, they are entirely different on their own.

Joy. A feeling of great pleasure and happiness. Joy is an attitude that defies circumstances. Happiness is a feeling based on circumstances. Joy is a state or condition. Happiness is simply an emotion. Joy can be constant whereas happiness is temporary. Joy is felt internally whilst happiness is felt externally.

Wanting what you have is joy. Having what you want is happiness. Joy is the cause, happiness is the effect. Happiness is a state of mind, joy is a mind-set. Joy comes when you make peace with who you are, how you are and why you are the way you are. Happiness is based on other people, things, places, thoughts and events.

You know when I first discovered this, it was all so mind-boggling to me. I, like yourself, believed they were one in the same. I didn't realize you needed one to feel the other. I realized you couldn't count on others to make you happy, that it had to be internal work and then you could add to that internal happiness. Little did I know, the internal feeling wasn't happiness, all along it was joy. Joy can last. Happiness can fizzle out.

Some people look for happiness in other things or what happens to them, instead they should be looking inward. External attainment does not bring real inner joy. So how do you find joy? Where do you begin?

In The Book Of Joy by the Dalai Lama and Desmond Tutu they outlined eight pillars of joy:

1. Perspective
2. Humility
3. Humor
4. Acceptance
5. Forgiveness
6. Gratitude
7. Compassion
8. Generosity

The common theme to feel joy seems to include putting others first.

Grounding yourself with prayer or meditation can help you tune inside deeper. Joy lives within you.

Some examples of happiness would include:

Going on a vacation, buying a house, ending up with your crush, getting that dream job, getting a new car and so on. The initial feeling of obtaining such things is happiness. The longer these things are in your possession the feeling of happiness towards them dwindles. It's why you shouldn't base your happiness on material things, the value of how they make you feel wears off over time.

Making and creating memories, on the other hand creates joy because they are only temporary. When you recall those memories, that feeling of joy comes flooding back, as they aren't permanent things and are only enjoyed for a small amount of time, such as going on a vacation. Typically, a vacation doesn't last much longer than a week, therefore the memories last and continue to bring you joy, unless of course you had a horrible time, which I'm hoping is not the case.

But joy is needed to have a fulfilled life. You need things that bring you joy. That continues to feed you joy. Many of us are feeling the crunch of the past couple of years and have forgotten what joy feels like. Being stuck in our houses brought on a whole other idea of routine and a different sort of lifestyle we weren't used to. Mindsets decreased and depression increased.

We weren't allowed to travel or visit friends and family. There was no making memories outside of the house or yard, so we had to get creative. Finding joy looked different for us all. I feel some of us are still trying to remember what used to bring us joy and try to implement those things back into our lives. Travel and society has somewhat returned to normal but there's still this darkness that lies over us all. Something that has sucked the joy and fun right out of us, allowing us to live in comfort and settling for what is. But, I don't want that for you. This is all about being joyful and feeling fulfilled, is it not? Isn't that why you're reading this?

Here's some simple ways to bring joy back into your life:

1) **Change your daily routine.** Incorporate something new and break out of the norm. Always wanted to be stronger or lose a little weight? Begin bringing in some form of daily movement like weight training or hiking.
2) **Surround yourself with positive people.** This one may seem obvious and don't we all want to only be surrounded

by positive people? Oh, what a perfect world it would then be, but sadly there are those who are not. WE must limit our time around them to truly feel joy.

3) **Let go of the past.** It's in the past for a reason. Reminiscing won't change a thing except how you feel. Most times, it makes us sad and depressed, especially if we think about good memories that are here and gone. They say there's a reason why the windshield is bigger than the rear-view mirror. Only more forward. Be done with the past and leave it where it belongs.
4) **Practice gratitude.** This one keeps popping up over and over and there's a reason for this. It's an important piece of a happy life. If you're not grateful for the little things you are already surrounded by, how are you able to welcome more of it into your life?
5) **Practice the law of attraction.** If you're unfamiliar with this philosophy, it's something you need to get on board with. Essentially, it states positive thoughts bring positive results whereas negative thoughts bring about negative outcomes. Which one will you be practicing?
6) **Give where you can.** When you give and help others it does create a feeling of joy. It's near impossible to not feel good when you're in the state of giving.
7) **Figure out your purpose.** Again, something else that has been mentioned a couple of times now. Another important piece of the complete puzzle. Knowing your purpose helps you serve others from your highest self.

A friend of mine summed it up best. When asked for a statement or philosophy that they could leave to their kids or that someone could take from their life they came up with the following. "Make sure you are happy. In all aspects of life and don't let anyone tell you what makes you happy." Well there! It always stuck with me though. They couldn't be right!

From Attitude to Gratitude

Since, I felt that gratitude, and your attitude were important, they get their own section. I'm sure with common sense you can see how they fit into the bigger picture and why they would be important in life. But, we're going to dive in a little deeper and break it down.

When you're in that "can do" attitude, you literally CAN DO anything. In fact, I've tried to teach my children that "can't" is a bad word and we should never use that term, because there always is a way. Sure, it may be harder or require more work, but there always is another way or another chance to try something again.

When we tell ourselves we "can't do" something we're essentially programming our brain to believe and chances are we'll give up before we really try. Again, the law of attraction works here. Positivity attracts positive results. If I believe I can, I will find a way or a path will make itself known to me. The universe, or whatever your belief is, works in mysterious ways. Something is always watching out and working for us, after all, we're all a bunch of energy just floating around.

If you're one of those that always finds themselves on the other side, thinking negatively and thinking everything bad always happens to them, then guess what you attract? That's right, more of that crap. Bad things will continue to happen to you whether you believe you're deserving of different or not. Even if you're a good person, what you think, you attract. This isn't just a theory, it's been backed by science.

Your attitude is also a reflection of how you view the world and your surroundings. Your attitude can have a negative or positive influence on your relationships, success, happiness, health, circumstances and well-being. You will either draw people towards you or repel the dependent on how your attitude is. No one enjoys being around someone who is constantly nagging, negative, hateful or rude. In all seriousness, why wouldn't you want to be the opposite?

Your attitude is an important factor in life and can influence your beliefs, moods, opinions and especially your emotions. It also reflects how you perceive the world around you and everything in it. By maintaining a positive attitude you can easily maintain stress levels and cope with challenges in a healthy manner.

Ways to maintain a positive attitude:

1) **Avoid gossiping.** We've all done it at one point or another, whether to this day or not you still do, now's the time for change. Gossiping only has a negative impact. Most gossip is not positive by any means. It also leads to higher stress and keeps you in a low vibrating mode. Plus, if you're surrounded by gossip, you're also not surrounded by people who will encourage you and help build you up. Wrong type of people to be around.
2) **Create a routine to follow.** Routines believe it or not. don't always mean boring. You can create a fun routine for yourself to follow, but something that keeps you focused and on the right track.

3) **Be mindful of your thoughts.** Are you beginning to lose focus and think negatively? Practicing mindfulness can significantly help you improve your ability to maintain that positive attitude that you're working towards creating.
4) **Treat yourself to some form of self-care.** I'm sure by now you've learnt how important taking care of yourself really is, if you didn't already know this. Caring for ourselves looks different for us all so do what feels best to you and brings you joy. How do you express love for yourself?
5) **Laugh more. Surround yourself with people who lift you up.** Watch comedy movies or sitcoms. Go to a dinner theatre. Read some jokes. Anything to make you laugh more. Bonus points for uncontrollable laughter.
6) **Have something to look forward to.** Are you beginning to see a lot of repeating? I hope it's beginning to stick. You should always have something you're working on or something to look forward to. Plan a trip. Action plan some steps for a goal you want to crush. Write a book. The options are endless.

Do you find it hard being grateful or does gratefulness come easy to you? Do you sometimes miss the little things in your life that you should be thankful are there? When the last time you expressed any gratitude towards someone? Do you feel you should be more grateful?

When you express gratitude, just like attitude, good things will come. Be grateful that you woke up another day. Be grateful for the warmth of the sun against your skin. Be grateful for you children's laughter, because it means they are happy. Be thankful for your hands that help you do things easily, even if you are a little shaky. If you really stop and look around, you will be able to find at least 10 things you are grateful for. If you really want to bring some effort forth, write them down in a gratitude journal.

According to a study done at Harvard University, being grateful makes you happier. When you're grateful, you acknowledge all the goodness in your life. Being grateful has also been said to help connect you with something larger than yourself, whether it's other people, nature or a higher power. Being grateful connects you to more positive emotions. It enables you to have better experiences, improves your health and helps build stronger relationships.

CHAPTER EIGHT

Habits and Routines

"Motivation is what gets you started. Habit is what keeps you going."

– Jim Rohn

Do you currently have a morning routine that consists of non-negotiables? Maybe you refuse to check your phone first thing in the morning until you've written in your gratitude journal. Speaking of that, if you don't have a gratitude journal, you really need to begin one. It's so refreshing to wake up in the morning and write five to ten things you are grateful for. Now I'm not talking about the big things, like family or a house to live in, although you should be very grateful for those things, I'm talking about the little things that you don't normally think about.

Are you grateful for a smooth commute on the way to work with very little to no traffic? Perhaps your coffee was made perfectly this morning and you enjoyed every mouthful. Did the Barista draw a heart in the foam on the top and did it make your day? Maybe you were grateful for a good night's sleep and you didn't wake up tired this morning. Perhaps, your crush smiled at you today and he has one of those smiles that makes you melt. Did the radio play "your jam" while you were on the road at some point throughout the day? I know when mine comes on, I crank the volume on high and I'm jamming. I don't care who sees.

There's many things in a run of a day to be grateful for. Be as specific as you can. This can be a hard exercise to do at first, but once you really sit down and put some thought into it, you won't be able to stop writing things down, guaranteed. Notice how you feel after you look back over your list.

Another great part of a morning routine is exercise. This is one of my non-negotiables. Lifting weights helps me release any stress I may be holding inside. I also love the endorphin rush that follows. Feeling stronger is always nice and the sense of accomplishment of not giving up on yourself is something to brag about. It can be very hard to incorporate exercise into a routine, especially if it's something you don't normally do. Building up discipline to all your excuses is a good start and that's another challenge we will get to as well. I'm not always disciplined but I'm all about not giving up on myself. I make no excuses when it comes to that, regardless of what the world is throwing at me.

Maybe a morning routine isn't something that works for you. Maybe you're more of an afternoon routine kind of person. Regardless, you should form some sort of routine that includes different forms of self-care. The exercise could be as easy as simply going for a ten minute walk or a short jaunt on the treadmill. Maybe in your journal you also write down things you'd like to accomplish. The trick is to write these down as though they have already happened. So, for example, by the time you're reading this book, I will be a best-selling author but at the current moment, I am not. I would write in my journal, "I am a best-selling author". Maybe you're an entrepreneur or hoping to start your own business. Maybe you want to gross $1,000,000 by the end of the year. All great goals, but they have to be written like they already happened. "I grossed $1,000,000 this calendar year." "I own my own business doing … (fill in the blank here)." You get the idea.

At first it may feel a little funny, almost as if you're lying to yourself because the things you're writing down having yet happened. Trust me, it does work. Eventually your "fake" beliefs will become reality. What I mean as in "fake" beliefs is you'll have a hard time believing any of it at first, until you cross one off the list, then two. It's good to do this over and over every day. I say write down ten things. Sounds like a lot, I know. Trust your mind will change throughout the days. They did for me anyways. I soon started crossing items off and had to find things to replace them or my mind changed and I realized I no longer wanted to reach some of those goals.

It becomes a lot of fun after a while. Brings you to dream land. You brainstorm a lot about all the fun things you could do with your life. It may also help you in finding your purpose. Your calling. Your why, if it's something you're unsure of what it is. Maybe you'll unpack some deep meaningful wants and needs you didn't even realize were there. I suggest you give it a try. Really just let your imagination flow. You'll be surprise at what comes up.

Habits and routines kind of go together. Once you create a routine, you must create a habit of being disciplined to stick with it. This habit can take some time to build, since it's new to you. At first you may forget about the new things you want to bring into your life. Over time, you'll get excited and look forward to your new routine it will just be a habit, like brushing your teeth is. Something you don't really need to think about, you just do it.

The problem with habits are that most of them have been instilled in us at a young age. We're used to doing something one way, or reacting a certain way, it can be hard to break out of. Not impossible, but challenging. Who doesn't love a good challenge though? I know I do. I'm always finding some sort of challenge for myself to do. One year I gave up junk food for an entire year. All of it. No chips, cake, donuts, cookies, candy, chocolate bars, you get the idea and that took some type of discipline I have never been faced with before. Well actually, that's not entirely true. I did also quit smoking cold turkey, without the aid of smoking replacement aids, just water and a lot of willpower apparently. I'm so very thankful till this day that I did.

Everything gets easier the longer you do it. It may seem near impossible at the start but it's because it's a new habit you're beginning to form and it comes with practice and a whole of discipline. Doing it on the days you're too tired or just aren't feeling it. You'd rather binge watch the latest show on Netflix that everyone has been talking about and it's a "must watch." Before you do, stop and think about why your routine or new habits that you are forming were important to you in the beginning. This is where having a very strong WHY, a reason why you must push through the suck and keep going.

Something else I do with my day is I participate in some form of personal-development. I highly recommend partaking in this. It could be in the form of listening to a motivational podcast, reading a book, watching an inspirational YouTube video or watching a TedX talk. There's so many platforms you could use. Maybe learning a new skill or taking a course is your form of self-care. Whatever it is, never stop learning. Always have a growth mindset. Always be open to new ideas.

One of my bad habits that I'm trying to work through is always catering to everyone else's needs and wants before my own. Now, don't get me wrong, there's absolutely nothing wrong with helping others and doing things they like, but when is it time for you? When do you take the time for yourself? To do something you love? Or should I say when you find the time. As a mother it doesn't always seem like there's much time for ourselves these days after we care for our families and look after the children. You deserve that hot bubble bath you've been dreaming of, uninterrupted. Maybe you want to curl up by the fire with a good book in your hands. That's right, this one! Hot cocoa with those tiny little marshmallows slowly melting on top. Sticky foam coating your top lip as you take a sip. You can almost picture it, it sounds so amazing.

It's very important for our well-being that we begin bringing ourselves into the picture daily. In order for us to be at our best to care for others, we also need to first take care of ourselves. End of story. By the end of this book, you should feel unstoppable and like nothing can hold you back from doing all the things. You'll be sent on the way with these tools you can take through life with you or lessons that you have learned. It'd be great if you even shared them with others when you see that they have made a difference in your life.

My goal for you is to feel unstoppable, accomplished, know what you need to do to feel fulfilled in life, more joyful. How to work through the pain and use it to create purpose. How to create new habits and get on with a routine. How not to overthink, unless it's really benefiting you. To ignore what the naysayers say, because they aren't going anywhere, you have to learn to live with them. How not to let external circumstances affect you in any way negatively. How to stop procrastinating. This is a big one for me. In fact, I'm so bad at it that I gave myself a deadline to finish this book in the next three days and I still have over 15,000 words to write. How's that for procrastination? Me and my silly deadlines. I did say I enjoy a good challenge.

So here I am up late after everyone's gone to sleep, writing my little heart out because I gave myself such a foolish timeline to write a book and get everything done for the launch date in three weeks. I leave no time for fucking around but I have done a lot of it, simply because I didn't build up the habit of writing everyday like I was planning to do in the very beginning. My routine got thrown off a couple of times with everyone being home and not having any quiet time to myself to write. I definitely find it easier to focus when it's quiet with easy listening music on. I wouldn't have to be up so late trying to reach a word count I had set for myself. I feel a lot of this is just foolish rambling, just to reach that point. Maybe I'll decide to leave it in the book, maybe I won't. Guess we'll see.

Are you seeing now the importance of habits and routines? I'm hoping so. If you can get one to stick, they will be very beneficial in the long run. You will be able to create more habits and routines where they are needed.

Now, I'm not talking about simply falling into the same routine you fall into day in and day out, that's what we're trying to work away from as you want an exciting life. It does help to have some sort of routine throughout your day to keep you heading on the path you're meant to follow.

Some reasons it's good to have a routine:

1) It helps decrease stress levels and has shown to improve mental health.
2) Better sleep patterns leave you feel more rested and relaxed.
3) Less anxiety.
4) Keeps us more focused and proficient.
5) Creates some sort of structure in your life allowing us to tackle the important tasks first.
6) Can save time if you know what already has to be done.
7) Helps us instill good habits and break bad ones.

Habit forming happens when you create a routine and consciously decide to continue to stick with it. Consistency is the secret when normalizing routines and habits. You have to continually remind yourself to do it again, again and again.

When I first got into exercise it took a couple of years for me to really incorporate a habit. There was times I'd workout for months straight and then I'd just stop. I hadn't done it long enough for it to stick. One day I just decided enough was enough and I had to make it work, no matter what.

Our most precious asset is our time. Once it is gone, it is non-retrievable. If you create some sort of routine you would actually free up some time that would otherwise be spent making decisions or planning. It helps us with using our time more efficiently.

Kick Procrastination In The Butt

It's one year from now and you are in the exact same place you were last year. How does this make you feel? Is this somewhere you want to be or were you hoping to be someplace else? What has procrastination cost you in your life up until this point? Think of the things you could have accomplished. Do you have a love of travelling? Think of the places you could have seen? A crush on someone? Think of the memories you could have made. Having money struggles? Think of the financial freedom you could have right now! Want to retire your parents? Need I continue on?

I'm sure by now you're feeling a bit of the crunch and pain from allowing procrastination to get in your way. I was extremely guilty of this. Hence, why I'm publishing a book at the age of 40 and not ten years ago. It's not a horrible thing to be this age and publishing a book. I have learned a thing or two I didn't know back then, however I feel I may have procrastinated on this a little longer than I should have. There was many times I could have been writing but instead found something else to do or distract me with.

So how exactly do you kick procrastination in the butt you may ask? Well first, I want you to sit in the pain you're feeling from allowing that part of the life you could have had be ripped from you. It's most certainly not too late to do any of the things you wanted to do, you just could have been doing them at this current moment.

I want you to write down, the things you were hoping to have accomplished by now that you feel by procrastinating may have taken from you. The cost of procrastination is the life you could have lived.

Let's have a look at some of the reasons on why we procrastinate in the first place:

1) **Lack of motivation.** If you don't feel compelled to do something you will resist doing it, it's that simple. Sadly, motivation is a temporary thing that's hard to create on your own. When you feel unmotivated you're less likely to do it and instead begin scrolling through social media, check emails or watch TV. Anything that's taking you away from what you know you should be doing.
2) **Feeling depressed or experiencing anxiety.** Suffering from either of those will not make you want to do anything.
3) **Low self-esteem.** Feeling like you're not good enough or unable to complete the task you need to.
4) **Bad sleep routine.** Getting enough sleep a night actually has a lot of good benefits.

So how can we kick procrastination in the butt?

Something I do when procrastination begins to creep in is I ask myself this simple question. "If I don't do this, what is it costing me?" I'm giving up on my future self, the self I want to become.

1) **You can simply ask yourself questions like I do.** What is this costing me?
2) **Practice self-compassion.** This one has come up quite a bit and there's a reason for this.
3) **Start off small.** If you have too many things at one time to accomplish, you'll end up doing none.
4) **Attach meaning.** Again, what's your why? If it's strong, even procrastination won't get in the way.

5) **Reward yourself.** You should always reward yourself, even if it's something small for reaching or completing the task at hand.

CHAPTER NINE

Live With No Regrets

"We should all start to live before we get too old. Fear is stupid. So are regrets."

– Marilyn Monroe

There was many times I have been faced with regret. The regrets of not doing something I wish I had done when I was younger. Regrets of not telling someone how I felt in fear of the feelings not being mutual or fear of being rejected. Regrets of not travelling a hell of a lot more when I was younger and not putting it off for over 14 years once I did begin travelling. Regrets of staying somewhere I wasn't appreciated or wanted longer than I should have whether that's at a job, friendship or relationship because it's been all of those for me at one point or another.

What I'm trying to say is, don't have any regrets, in life. Ever. Sure, sometimes the outcome won't be what we were expecting or hoping but what if it does work out? What if the outcome is better than you had hoped? You'll never know if you don't just take that chance. Take that leap when you're afraid to jump.

Trust me the regret of not doing something you wish you would have will eat at you, for days. Sometimes even months. Don't waste any time or all you'll end up with is a bunch of missed opportunities. Missed opportunities really hit you hard. You never know the last conversation you'll have with someone or the last time you're being held in their arms, pulled in hard against them.

Think about how it'd feel, the last time you hug your children. That time they hung up on you because they were mad and you should have called them back and said you were sorry and you loved them but you never got the opportunity because something tragic happened. Maybe they were off to a party you had no idea about and one of their friends were drinking and they crashed and never got to say the things you wanted to say.

Think about all the relationships or marriages you were in. Crushes you had on people. All the amazing memories you created with them, never expecting the time to come to end. Then sometimes it did. Sometimes without reason. Or so it felt anyways. Everything was going good, or so you thought, but someone else came into the picture and you were no longer a thought. So easily disposable. Or maybe some anger and hatred entered the picture making you feel useless, weak and feeling like a nobody.

Embrace every moment with everybody. Never hold back the chance to say what's on your mind or heart, you may just lose the chance. If you love someone, tell them. What's the worst that can happen? They don't say it back because they don't quite feel the same way, yet. Doesn't mean that they won't in the future.

What if they did say it back? Imagine how that would make you feel. On cloud nine I bet. Now, imagine you didn't say it and its months down the road and you're no longer in each other's lives but you can't stop thinking of them and wish you would have just told them how you felt, maybe things would be different now. Maybe, they wouldn't have moved onto someone else who wasn't afraid to express their feelings for them. No regrets.

Are you feeling any pangs in the pit of your stomach yet? Can you think back to a time you held yourself back from something because you were afraid of the outcome? We all have. You're for sure not alone. However, regretting doing or not doing something is a horrible feeling and I don't want you to have to feel it anymore. I want to give you some tools to use so you live a fulfilling life with no regrets. Sure, we can also regrets things we have done, but we can't change those. Those are in the past and the past can't be changed nor should they be regrets, as at one point they were something that you had wanted.

But really, just sit and think about it for a moment. I'm sure something has come up for you while reading this that you regret not doing. Maybe you've always wanted to write a book, but never had. It's never too late and there's no time like the present! Maybe you regret the last conversation you had with someone and they are no longer here to be able to make things right. Maybe you regret not spending more time with your grandparents or parents even, before they passed. If they are still alive now, go call them. Go visit them. Don't waste any time. If you're currently on bad terms, make up with them. If they've hurt you in anyway, forgive them for wronging you and let it go. You don't have to forget the hurt, but you need to forgive them, whether they apologize or not, so you can heal and move past it and enjoy what time you do have left.

Are you kids still young and living at home? Growing up fast aren't they? Soon they will be teenagers and not wanting to spend as much time with you anymore. Or they will move away to a university that's in a different province, state or even country. Make time to spend with them. Enjoy all the stages. Enjoy the sleepless nights, the times they call for you when you feel bothered. There will be a time it all stops and you'll do anything to want it hit rewind to have some more time. No regrets. Don't set yourself up to be able to have regrets.

Here's a couple other ways to ensure you live a life with no regrets:

1) **Let go of the past.** It's gone. We all have regrets there and unless there's something you can do to change it now, let it go. Easier said than done, I know, but sometimes your own peace is more important. If you can fix a regret from the past, then Go For It!!
2) **Forgive.** This has been mentioned previously, I know and sometimes it's a hard thing to do, especially if you feel like you've been wrong, have unanswered questions or are confused about certain things that have happened, but holding on to the pain is only going to make you feel worse and ruin your peace. So forgive, let go and move on.
3) **Be more aware.** Pay closer attention to the things in your life. People who are important to you. Make the time to see them, go for coffee maybe talk and catch up. Pay attention to what scares you and makes you feel uneasy, you may regret not doing the thing, so do it anyways. Do it scared. Eventually it will get easier.

4) **Learn to practice gratitude.** What are you thankful? What memories, experiences and people have made your life pretty great? Reflect on those.
5) **Find your purpose.** I'm sure you're really beginning to see a pattern here and how everything ties together to live that big life you're dreaming of. When you're working on your purpose, there are no regrets. You will only regret not working towards it.
6) **Take good care of yourself.** Mentally and physically. If you're depressed, burnt out or worn down, you can't serve at your best or be there for others, which means everything gets pushed to the wayside and nothing is important. Once you get out of that funk, you'll have a pile of regrets. Don't waste that time. Take care of yourself now. Seek professional help if that's what you require. There is no shame.
7) **Bye, bye comfort zone.** This one should be a given and clearly when you do the things that scare you, you have no regrets. Stepping out of your comfort zone is a great place to start!

Do we feel stuck with uncertain the path that we should be taking? Is it because we feel stuck, we're uncertain what the next step is to take or where to begin. I refuse to get to the end of my life and have things I never got to accomplish because I allowed to hold myself back, in whatever form that may be. There's always something intimidating about the unbeaten path. The uncertainty. The urgency to have clarity. We have to look beyond that, for that's where our greatness lies.

Love

"Joy is the evidence of inner growth." – Maria Montessori

I'd be lying to you if I told you that you can live a fulfilled life without love. Clearly, you can live an incredible life without love, especially if you're single, don't get me wrong. There will be a day that comes though that you're going to want someone to share your life with. Make memories with.

Now, there's different types of love, like love we give and receive from our children, siblings, family, friends, and love we have with our partners. Then there's self-love that we have for ourselves. I feel they all play a pretty important role in living your best life.

There's so many studies and controversies around this topic and whether it is truly something needed in life. You can be completely happy on your own and with what you have, but at some point or another you will begin to feel alone. You will crave that special bond you create with someone. The intimacy and passion you share with your "supposed person". Feeling like we truly matter to someone. Being admired and appreciated. Finding your best friend to do life with.

The question lies within do we all really only have that "one person" for us or do we build with someone we have a connection with into that person? Could there more than one person out there for each of us? Love is a funny thing.

It can also be falsely disguised as lust or infatuation. Those intense feelings in the beginning you share with someone. You know, those ones you think are "love at first sight"? That's not to say you can't share an incredible bond with someone in the early stages, but is it love? Most likely no.

Love grows over time. When you begin learning about one another. The good, bad and ugly. You see their flaws and still want them a part of your life. They upset you or make you angry, yet you forgive them and continue to keep them around. This is where love blossoms. When you know so much about the other person that them being a part of you just make sense. You share common interests but are also okay doing your own things. When you can't imagine life without them, this is love. Or a very unhealthy attachment style.

One thing that became apparent to me and this actually hit me during my grandmother's 90th birthday celebration, (Yes, I said 90!) is that it's not about the people you know, it's about the lives you've impacted along the way. The amount of family and friends that came out that day to show my Nan some love and help her celebrate that milestone of a day, was unspeakable. Everyone from the town crier to the church choir was there.

Over the decades of her life she had shown compassion to everyone that crossed her path. She had developed many long term friendships and never let life slow her down, even though it had tried a couple of times and failed. She had travelled to many places and was always up for the next adventure, and still is for the most part.

Her life has never been conflicted with social media. I'm not even sure if she knows what Facebook even is. She doesn't get consumed with the news and loves to get lost in a good book. She's always happy and positive and gives back to her community. She finds the greatness is every day and always was such a strong willed lady.

She's the prime example of what living your best life looks like. No, I'm not only saying any of this because she's going to be reading my book, (Hi Nan! Love you!) but because I truly wanted to give you an example of it being done and show you, that it is possible for you as well. It's possible for us all.

So, is love in your life important? Studies have shown that being in love, or feeling love, releases our feel good hormones as well as triggers the neuro-chemicals that increase positivity. Sounds important enough to me. Who wouldn't want to feel that amazing?

CHAPTER TEN

What's Life Without A Little Fun?

"Joy is the evidence of inner growth."
– Maria Montessori

Fun! Life would sure be a big ball of blah if we didn't add some fun into the mix, am I right? It gives us a chance to let loose and really enjoy ourselves. It also gives us something to look forward to so life doesn't become stagnant, very mediocre. We all know how I feel about mediocrity, now don't we. I know when covid hit, the world looked a little different. We were all derived of having fun. It was more difficult to be able to leave our house and do what we used to do. Thankfully, the world have begun to return to a state of normalcy.

What's the last thing you can remember you did that was fun? When was the last time you had something fun planned to look forward to? Now, I understand with the restrictions that have been on and off in the past few years may have reflected and put restraints on the things we were allowed to do, but how about now?

I used to love travelling. Seeing new places. Trying new food. Meeting new people. Making new memories. Creating new adventures. I still love travelling and I will continue doing it again soon enough. In fact, I had a trip planned for Hawaii in May 2019. Hawaii of all places! Covid arrived that March and shut everything down. So close to laying under my palm trees once again. I am determined to make it there one day. I've also had a couple of trips to Punta Cana cancelled and one to St. Louis. Hopefully Texas will be a go this June for the huge health coaching conference. Travelling is life.

For now, I'll have fun locally. Most time that involves spending time on the sailboat and exploring islands or taking a stroll downtown in our capital city, walking on the waterfront checking out local businesses and grabbing an ice cream. It's the small moments in life that matter most and the people you create memories with.

If you're unsure on how to add some fun into your life or maybe you're looking for some new ideas, check these out:

1) **Pet sit for someone or adopt a pet.** New pets can bring lots of love, fun and joy into our lives. Don't forget they also add to your current responsibilities.
2) **Explore somewhere new.** Whether that's locally or abroad. Alone or with someone else.
3) **Change it up.** Spice up your routine a bit. Add something to it. Do it out of order. Break away from the normalization of every day.

4) **Try a new food or check out a new restaurant.** Indulge in something you don't usually. Life's too short, eat the cake.
5) **Have a party or go to one.** Gather some friends and family and have a bonfire and maybe a couple drinks. Potlucks are always fun!
6) **Go see you favorite band live, again.** Concerts are always all the hype. It's hard to break free from the energy of that many people in one area.
7) **Treat yourself.** You derserve it. You've worked hard at living your best life.

Good time keep our power and energy high. It keeps us feeling alive. After all, isn't that what we all want to feel? High on life and happy!

Keep Emotions at Bay

Emotions, aren't they a funny thing? Sometimes we allow our emotions to control a situation over logic. It's not hard to get caught up in certain moments that fog our thinking over. Even if we know it's not right for us, our judgement can be impaired based on how we're feeling. Think about a time you were very easily angered and how you may have overreacted and then when you cooled down, you knew you lost your cool and it could have been prevented if some thinking had first taken place. Maybe even a time you crushed on someone you knew wasn't good for you but you just couldn't pull away from the feeling. We've all experience it, it's inevitable. We've all been through times when logic would have been a better play than allowing our emotions take over. It's a deadly game if you ask me.

I originally wanted to write this book because I knew there had to be more to life than what my current life had looked like. I was constantly living in my emotions. Living with trauma and no matter how often I tried to break free from it, something always pulled me back in. I have good and bad days like everyone else. I knew others were feeling the same way I was because I was seeing it all around me. In person and on social media. No one was happy and no one was living and feeling fulfilled anymore. There had to be another way to live life. That's when it hit me. I had to figure this out and help others.

I really wanted to dive deep into the things that matter, well matter to me anyways, with living your best life. Now, I know there will be those things that you disagree with in this book and that's fine. Everyone is entitled to their own opinion, I just hope you find something in here that helped steer you in the direction you were trying to go or help you out of a sticky situation. If you find one thing useful, then I have succeeded.

Emotions, you can feel them. Really dig deep and let them take over. Sit on the bathroom floor and let out that ugly cry with your glass of wine, yelling at the top of your lungs to let all the frustration out. Surrounding yourself with used tissue you throw down beside you. Feel everything. Then get up, clean yourself off. Have a nice hot bath or shower. Do you hair and make-up. Put on your kick ass bitch boots or outfit and look at yourself in the mirror and tell that bad bitch that you are, that you are deserving of a life full of love, happiness, success and freedom. Blow yourself a kiss and walk away.

Whatever you do, don't stay in your emotions. They will eat you alive. I know firsthand. They will take over every aspect of your life. You will have to acknowledge them, feel them but don't stay in them. This is so very important and what I have done wrong and allowed myself to get lost in.

The habits you have created through your life will continue to be the ones you follow unless you decide to change them. Living in your emotions is one of them. This can be a hard feat. It's like teaching a dog new tricks, as the saying goes. Your old habits, that are no longer serving you, are programed into your subconscious, so you do them automatically without thinking. If you're not living the life that you want, your habits are not working for you and it's time to create some new ones.

Say you want to begin working out, well if you're in the habit of sleeping in later in the mornings, this will be a new thing for you if you plan to get up earlier to incorporate this new habit into your life. Even just fitting it in in the evening is the beginning of changing your routine.

It can take some time, but it's not impossible. Eventually over time, it will just be a part of your day, you won't even think about it anymore and it won't be such a big deal. Start with a small change, daily. It takes 21 days to create a habit and 90 days for it to stick and be second nature. This can also count towards dealing with you emotions. You can learn to control them.

I know not everyone reading this book has children but mine, they are the reason I had taken the leap and did everything I had to do to make this possible. I wanted to be more than their mom. I wanted to be a legacy and pave the way for them. Show them that anything they dream, no matter how big, they can accomplish. That regardless of all the dark times they will face in life, I will always be with them. There will always be a piece of me I left behind for them, that they can pass on to their children.

I just want them to have the best life they possible can. I want them to know that it's entirely possible and I will begin with showing them that it is. I have held myself back for far too long. I have allowed others to hold me back. It's my time to shine. I'm the only one that can allow myself this gift. The opportunity to shine. Having external support to guide me helps tremendously but I have to do it from the inside in. I have to feel all the feelings. The good, bad and ugly and learn from each one.

While writing this book I experienced a few cases of writers block. A couple of times I had to ask myself some questions. What is it that I want to tell these people? How can I help them? What is it that they struggle with? What is it that I struggle or have struggled with that I can help them?

For me, when I thought about living my best life, it brought me back to a time when I was young, when no dream felt off the table or too big. When it felt okay to dream. As you get older, you become conditioned more on how you should feel, or what you should do or feeling that the path you'd like to take is stupid because your friends aren't doing it, or no one understands why I want to do this.

It's only for you to understand the decisions you make. You know what makes you happy and fulfilled. No one else can do that for you. When you're a kid, the options feel endless. Your imagination runs wild with thoughts and ideas. Why is that so frowned upon as you age? It should be encouraged! Think back to what you wanted to me when you were young. Is that something you'd like to do now? Even before having kids, we all enjoyed and loved doing things. Are these still things you enjoy now and miss doing?

We do seem to lose ourselves as we age. I think this is where the term "mid-life crisis" kicks in. When you get to a point in your life, usually what you consider mid age, and look back at all the unaccomplished goals you wanted to achieve. You feel like death is now closer than your youth and you want to begin living life, your way. You want to do all the things you thought you had time for and have now slowly began realizing that time isn't promised. You have so much that you want to life for. It's like realization kicks in.

This is when most people begin picking up a workout routine or leave their marriages because they realize they are unhappy. They begin travelling and seeing the world, or maybe they write a book. Ha! Travelling is next on my list. I live and breathe writing and travel. I really need to combine the two.

qSit on the sand in front of my beach house, underneath the palm trees, laptop on my lap, typing away, writing book number, who knows what. My kids, now gown teenagers playing volleyball or splashing in the water. One of my girls is a water bug, but only as of late. She never really used to care for the water. I have a margarita in hand, because as the saying goes, "Write drunk, edit sober." My mentor shared that one with me and it just stuck. Most times I had a coffee close by when I was writing, over anything else. A drink does go down nicely though, once and a while. A laptop pairs nicely with a glass of fine Italian wine.

Where am I going with this chapter that has been rambling on, not making much sense and all over the place? Simply put. Life is too short. Time isn't promise and do whatever it takes to live the life you see yourself living. Mic drop. Okay, okay. I know you know this. You need help getting there and this is where I come in. This is why you picked up this book in the first place.

Looking for some answers. Some guidance. Some actionable steps to getting there. Believe me, it's coming. We're going to cover all the things.

I can vision, me having to write a second book as I'm not going to be able to share and say everything I'm going to want to say in this one book. There's just so many things to touch on when it comes to living your best life. Every time I think I have it figured out, something else comes to mind that seems important when it comes to life and the best one you can live.

At first, I thought it was all about mindset. Okay, you have to get your mindset right and then everything else will fall into place. Then I realized that it wasn't true and there was more to it than that. Also, how do you get your mindset right. I also figured that if you vibrate and work from a high frequency you attract and if you work and radiate from a lower frequency you repel. But, it didn't stop there. You need to feel some sense of joy or happiness to feel fulfilled. You can't appreciate that from a place of sadness or anger. You just stay down where it keeps you. I'll show you tools later on that help you get out of the repeating loop.

Love, it felt like it was needed to live your best life but I'm still up in the air about this one. It's important and we all want to feel a sense of belonging and like we matter but I also feel like you can work towards living your best life and welcome that later on. Maybe it's needed for the complete picture. That perfect life. I really hate saying that because nothing really is ever perfect. Just that life you pictured for yourself. Having someone to confide in and talk about your day with. Someone that just makes sense for you. You should never allow external circumstances to dictate your happiness or worthiness but it's nice when someone helps boosts those things that you've already created on your own.

Becoming unstoppable looks very different for us all. For some they may feel as though they have to have a loving and understanding partner by their side to feel unstoppable. For others it could be conquering something they were always afraid of. Whatever that looks like for you, figure things out and crush the life you were meant to live!

This novel is compiled of the things I have felt necessary to live a fulfilled life. Some you may agree with, others you may not. Use the tactics I have shared in the areas of life you feel are pertained towards the life you are after. If you already feel unstoppable and are living a very fulfilling life, please feel free to share with me the things you feel are important to you. We can all learn from one another.

You really, really, really can't allow your emotions to take over because it can and will ruin you. I'm a Taurus and we're all about the emotions and feelings, so for me it was always a huge challenge to try and control them. It's still something I struggle with to this day.

At the end of your life you will be more disappointed by the things that you didn't do than the things you did do. Even if some things didn't turn out as we were hoping. You never want to spend any of your days wondering "what if". Just do it, then you'll know. Maybe something incredible will come of it. Something better than you could have ever imagined.

One of my biggest challenges that I'm working on overcoming and perhaps this is something you need to work on as well is removing my expectations of others. The more I seem to expect a certain thing or outcome from someone, the more disappointed I seem to end up. You see, we can't control any other person. Not their thoughts, actions or words. The only control we have is how we react.

We can't make someone else like us. We can't place expectations on getting a certain job. We can put our absolute best foot forward, prepare for it and maybe even add in a twist of manifesting, if that's your thing, to encourage the desired outcome but sometimes it just doesn't happen. Sometimes there's a plot twist. Typically, it's because we're being prepared for something better than we could have imagined.

What's the worst that could happen? You're heartbroken for a bit. You're sad and you feel like your worthless and not deserving of the things you want. But, what if for a minute you could see into the future and see a relationship more suited to your needs and a career that was ten times better and something you didn't even imagine seeing yourself doing, would it be worth all the rejection? Would it not seem as terrible and you wouldn't mind going through it if the desired outcome was even greater?

Of course not! The thing is, the outcome will be better than expected. You just have to believe it will be. It has been backed by science that positive energy draws in positive energy and amazing things so the best thing for you to do when disappointment happens to is remain in your power as best you can, after you feel all the emotions, and then get back to work. The more you work on yourself, the more the universe will reward you.

It's really hard sometimes to see all of this when you're in the moment, but it does happen. The secret is grounding yourself before you try to practice any of the techniques I have shared in this book. Nothing will work if you're trying them from a place of sadness, anger or resentment. If you're feeling triggered or distracted by something else, they will be harder to apply. The secret is to get yourself to a place where you can begin practicing and incorporating new habits.

Your daily life is set up based on a series of habits you have built over the course of your life. You become comfortable once you have established a routine and that's the reason why many of us feel stuck and unhappy. Breaking free from this and incorporating things that challenge you or scare you will create new and better habits. Stepping away from your comfort zone is where you grow.

Life is about being happy. Doing what makes you happy. It doesn't have to make sense to anyone else. If you're not happy, you can't deliver from your highest power. You won't be able to take care and help others. You won't be in the right state of mind to crush your goals. You won't step out of your comfort zone and do all the things. Want to hike Mt. Kilimanjaro? You can't do that in a state of unhappiness. Well, I guess I shouldn't say you can't, you most certainly can BUT perhaps you won't find the purpose in the journey or even make it to the top. You may just give up part way, and besides, what enjoyment would it be if you were unhappy doing something you dreamt about accomplishing?

Being grateful ties into being happy. When you're grateful for what's already around you, greater things happen. You attract more into your life. You see things from a different angle. Everything becomes clearer. You can accomplish goals.

You must be grateful for the good and bad. The bad things in life happen to teach us lessons. Sometimes we can't always see at the moment what it's teaching us but in time, the answer will become clearer.

No one can love you better than yourself. Only you know what's best for you. Only you know what's hurting you or pushing you further from your goals and dreams. Why would you want anything but the best for yourself? Sometimes we have to let people go, not because we want to always but because they drain our soul or energy or you're on different paths in life. This can be a painful process, especially if you thought they'd be in your life for a long time, or longer than they were.

Living you best life starts with healing. Deep, internal healing of your body and mind. Whatever it is that you believe in whether it's God, the universe or something else, it will present to you, what you give out. If you're constantly in a state of sorrow and sadness, that's all you will feel. That's all you will get in return. There comes a time when you have to say "enough is enough" and brush yourself off and live the BEST FUCKING LIFE that you possible can. You don't have time to waste on being sad or angry. Life is all about happiness, joy and abundance. You want to travel? Find a way to make it happen, Don't waste any more time wishing. Wishing for something is not taking action and getting it. This is your wake up call. You must find a way.

You can have anything in this life that you want. It may not be at the exact time that you're hoping for it, but it will come to you when you're ready to receive. You also must be careful, because you can easily lose that very thing if you take advantage of it, if you don't enjoy it while you have it. Just because you got the very thing you wanted, nothing in life is forever, so you never know how long it's here to stay.

I was once reminded of this by two words someone had said to me "just enjoy." At the time, I was in a different place. Always rushing towards the next thing and not being in the current moment. Learning the hard way by losing things and people very important to me to enjoy everything as you have it. I even had the two words tattooed on my arm.

There has been many a times I felt alone and lost. I'd wasted too many years of my life on people who weren't afraid to lose me. That's when loving myself, taking care of myself and bettering myself became important. I decided to do for me and begin working on the things I always wanted to accomplish in life. I was only in the game for myself. It was me against me. I have no competition, only who I was yesterday and today. Now, I'm a fucking legend. Hear me roar!!

CONCLUSION

How do you really live your best life?

"I choose to make the rest of my life, the best of my life."
– Louise Hay

When you look at the grand scheme of it all, there's so many things that living your best life can include. There's things I'm sure that I hadn't even mentioned. Here's a nice list I made easy for you to find if you're looking for a quick reference sometime.

If you don't get your mind right, you will lose every time. Master your mind and that little voice that loves to protect you.

Make sure you're always having fun in some way. Don't take everything so seriously.

Find a reason to laugh or smile every day.

Have something to look forward to. This is where having a goal or dream to chase comes in handy. Have a trip coming up? Seeing a friend you haven't seen in years?

Stay away from negativity as best you can. Surround yourself with people who possess the mindset and attitude that you have or are striving for.

Don't let your emotions take over, they will always win.

Learn to overcome or control self-doubt, limiting beliefs, overthinking and all those not so fun things.

Be grateful. Keep a gratitude journal.

Help others. Whatever that looks like for you.

Learn to slow down and just enjoy every moment and the journey through life. We're only here for a short time so we have to make the most of it.

Learn how to fight against distractions and develop focus.

Learn to overcome laziness and procrastination. What has it robbed you of so far in your life? Are you in the same spot you were a year ago? Five years from now, do you still want to be there?

Workout – Look better and feel better. Have more energy, it's a win-win. Along with all the health benefits that arise from it.

Do what you say you're going to do – Accomplish your goals.

Learn not to give a fuck. When you don't care or react to BS, you'll in the end feel happier.

Start building your future. Do it alone, scared, broke, just do it.

Control your actions and reactions. Some things you can't control but you can always control how you react.

Compete with no one. Just be better than you were yesterday.

Find a way to be hungry for what's next.

Be passionate about what you do. Growth comes from conquering our fears. Our next level lives on the other side of what we fear the most.

Courage is moving forward even though you're afraid anyways. Take the uncomfortable action.

On the other side of temporary pain, you meet your other self.

Don't wait for trauma or something major to happen to convince you it's time to live your best life. Do it now before you lose the chance.

Remove your glass ceiling.

Stop half assing your life. Be persistent. Be relentless.

Never give up. Strive for more.

If you put your happiness in the hands of others, you will end up being disappointed. Create your own and welcome others into your world.

Learn how to step into your power and own who you are.

Build healthy habits that you can do daily.

Invest in yourself.

Learn to set boundaries and stick with them.

Live for you. No one else understands your wants and needs. They don't understand your soul purpose.

Get honest with yourself.

Do yourself a favour and take action.

Stop overthinking.

Turn pain into purpose.

Never stop dancing.

Expect there will be disappoinments and how to use them to grow.

Love unconditionally and wholeheartedly.

Say what's on your heart, before you lose the time.

Spend quality time with friends and family.

Never take your time for granted. Use it wisely.

All you have is right now. Yesterday is gone and tomorrow isn't here yet. Stay focused on the present moment.

Acknowledgments

First and foremost I want to thank you, the reader. The one who took the time to purchase my book and read it in its entirety. I hope you were able to find some of its contents useful and you will put them to good practice towards living your greatest life.

Thank you to my daughters Dakota and Hailey. You always have been my biggest fans and believed in me when I had a hard time believing in myself. You've shown me that it's okay to dream big and just enjoy life. You've given me strength on the days I needed it and you make life so worthwhile. Oh, the adventures that await us!

To Russell, thank you for being my rock when I needed someone to lean on, for supporting me on my endeavours and for putting up with my crap for all these years and still loving me like when we first met.

To Codey, the son I never had to birth. Thank you for showing me what motherhood was all about before Dakota and Hailey came along. Thanks for being the best brother they could ever ask for and for setting good examples for them along the way. It made my life a little easier.

Thank you to my daughter in law Cassie and granddaughter Adalia, for always being so loving and accepting and just being yourselves. Thank you for bringing little Dali into the world to give my heart someone else to love.

Thank you to my mom, Brenda. Who has only ever wanted the best for me and would give the shirt off her back to help anyone. She's the supermom of Moms! She's always been so supportive and loving and knows how to always add in some fun. She's always been my role model when it came to being a mother and she has taught me so much about life.

Thank you to my three sisters, Nicolle, Alisha and Tari. Wow! We've had our fair share of ups and downs over the years but don't all siblings? You three have always been the first I came to when I needed someone to talk to. You've helped me through some pretty tough times. You all always know what to say and how to cheer me up. You've been my strength when I had none, my shoulder to cry on and the whisper in my ear.

Thank you to my Dad, Stanley, for being a good father and helping guide me on my way as I set out in life as a young woman.

A big thanks to my grandmother, Helen, for leading the way and setting an example for us all, showing how life should be lived.

Thank you to all my incredible friends, there's too many of you to name, but you know who you are. Thank you for all the amazing adventures, fun times, laughter, supporting me and loving me for my crazy self.

Huge thanks to my mentor, Mirav, for seeing potential in me and not allowing me to give up on myself. For kicking my ass when it needed to be done and for paving the way on being a best-selling author and publisher. Thanks for all your knowledge and support and for believing in me. I know I would have eventually figured all this out one day, but without you, I don't feel it would have happened this soon.

Thank you to my amazing community of friends whom are also becoming best-selling authors. You ladies have shown me so much love and support and I'm so thankful to call you all friends.

Thank you to Rob Elliott, for taking some time out of your busy life to schedule in an interview. I am looking extremely forward to working with an inspiring guy such as yourself.

Thank you to my life coach Angie, for getting the ball rolling on this and helping me get out of the funk I was in. I was at the lowest of my lows and you helped me see the light again and encouraged me to begin writing this novel.

Thank you to anyone else I may have missed. There is so many of you I personally want to thank but it's so hard to name you all. So many of you have supported me, shown me love and helped me out in one way or another. So thank very much from the bottom of my heart.

About the Author

Laura Berggren is a health and wellness coach who also has a love of writing. When not helping others on their fitness journeys, she can be found on her family's sailboat, hiking back to a remote cabin or camping. She lives in Nova Scotia, Canada with her spouse Russell, two daughters Dakota and Hailey, dog Xander, cat Lily, two guinea pigs, nine hens and four roos, one being a silkie named Elvis.

Manufactured by Amazon.ca
Bolton, ON

30811777R00074